from

to

BIG
IDEA
BOOK

Jessie L. Kwak

Create a Writing Practice That You Brings Joy

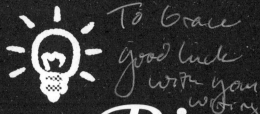

To Grace
Good luck
with your
writing!

From Big Idea to Book

Create a Writing Practice That Brings You Joy

Jessie L. Kwak

Microcosm Publishing
Portland, OR

Kwak

FROM BIG IDEA TO BOOK
Create a Writing Practice That Brings You Joy

Part of the Good Life Series
© Jessie L Kwak, 2022
This edition © Microcosm Publishing, 2022
First Edition, 3,000 copies
First published March 8, 2022
ISBN 9781648410628
This is Microcosm #603
Cover illustration by Lindsey Cleworth
Book design by Joe Biel

For a catalog, write or visit:
Microcosm Publishing
2752 N Williams Ave.
Portland, OR 97227
(503)799-2698
Microcosm.Pub/BigIdeaBook

To join the ranks of high-class stores that feature Microcosm titles, talk to your rep: In the U.S. **Como** (Atlantic), **Fujii** (Midwest), **Book Travelers West** (Pacific), **Turnaround** in Europe, **Manda/UTP** in Canada, **New South** in Australia, and **GPS** in Asia, India, Africa, and South America. We are sold in the gift market by **Faire**.

Did you know that you can buy our books directly from us at sliding scale rates? Support a small, independent publisher and pay less than Amazon's price at **Microcosm.Pub**

Global labor conditions are bad, and our roots in industrial Cleveland in the 70s and 80s made us appreciate the need to treat workers right. Therefore, our books are MADE IN THE USA.

Library of Congress Cataloging-in-Publication Data

Names: Kwak, Jessie L., author.
Title: From big idea to book : create a writing practice that brings you
    joy / by Jessie L. Kwak.
Description: Portland, OR : Microcosm Publishing, [2022] | Summary: "Want
    to write a book? Half the battle is finding a practice that works for
    you. Successful author and creativity expert Jessie Kwak is here to help
    you do just that-and have fun doing it. In her view, every part of the
    process is important: idea generation, development, research, planning,
    drafting, revising, and publication are all covered here in
    friendly, accessible detail. As in her previous book, From Chaos to
    Creativity, Kwak helps you set up a system that makes the most of your
    creative ideas and helps them find their best form-and their audience.
    Fiction and nonfiction writers alike can use this book as a muse, a
    checklist, and a resource for getting your ideas out of your head and
    into the world"-- Provided by publisher.
Identifiers: LCCN 2021052742 | ISBN 9781648410628 (trade paperback)
Subjects: LCSH: Authorship. | Writing--Technique. | Creation (Literary,
    artistic, etc.)
Classification: LCC PN145 .K93 2022 | DDC 808.02--dc23/eng/20211206
LC record available at https://lccn.loc.gov/2021052742

MICROCOSM · PUBLISHING

Microcosm *Publishing* is Portland's most diversified publishing house and distributor with a focus on the colorful, authentic, and empowering. Our books and zines have put your power in your hands since 1996, equipping readers to make positive changes in their lives and in the world around them. Microcosm emphasizes skill-building, showing hidden histories, and fostering creativity through challenging conventional publishing wisdom with books and bookettes about DIY skills, food, bicycling, gender, self-care, and social justice. What was once a distro and record label was started by Joe Biel in his bedroom and has become among the oldest independent publishing houses in Portland, OR. We are a politically moderate, centrist publisher in a world that has inched to the right for the past 80 years.

TABLE OF CONTENTS

Part Four: What's Next? • 177

Put It Out There • 181

Resources • 187

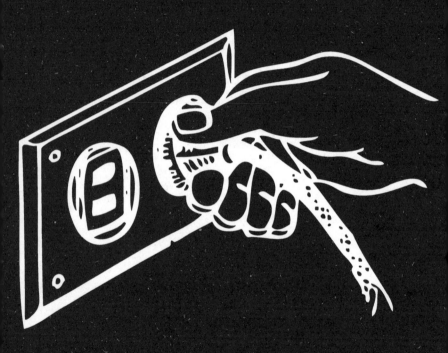

FOREWORD

The book you're now reading is the book I wish I would've had when I started my public writing career almost fifteen years ago. Jessie does a masterful job of demystifying all parts of the book publishing process, and I suspect it'll be a guide that we readers will be turning to time and time again.

And, while I'm letting you know what you're getting into, I'll also set you up to not be as surprised by Jessie as I was when I met her a few years ago. We first met because a client asked her to interview me for the upcoming launch of my book, *Start Finishing*. I'd worked with ghostwriters before, so I expected that there'd be a healthy amount of corrections and edits to make to the write-up of the interview. I slotted the requisite amount of time to address the anticipated corrections and edits only to find that there were a handful of small edits that were mostly idiosyncratic preferences. I had to reread the piece several times because, surely, I'd missed something.

The only thing I missed was how excellent Jessie is at what she does. I later contacted her to help me get some articles done when I was in the crunch of the launch, and each article had the same level of quality. I started referring her to clients and they had the same delightful surprise, even though I told them to be prepared for her to nail their voice and content.

I later discovered that she was a prolific nonfiction and fiction author, as well. She's that rare breed of writer who can nail writing for others, writing nonfiction, and writing fiction. I've long wondered how she pulls it off; the contents of this book reveal the structures and practices that channel her magic.

Since Jessie so ably addresses the structures and practices that will help you go from idea to book, I want to touch on the magical side of writing books. My dear friend and author of multiple best sellers, Susan Piver, once shared a quote she got from Julia Cameron: "The first rule of magic is containment."

Maybe you find the magic in wonder. Perhaps it's the spark of service to help someone. Perhaps it's a character or set of characters who take on a life of their own and surprise you as you're writing. Perhaps it's that feeling of finally being able to articulate the simple insight that's been vexing you for years.

I've seen too many of my friends, clients, and colleagues get stuck with their book because they've lost the magic. A consistent cadence of writing, talking with friends, and getting readers—all things Jessie covers—help you to stay in touch with the fire and magic of creativity. That's the "containment" part of Cameron's quote.

But without the magic, there's nothing to contain.

Fortunately, it's not the magic that disappears, but your connection to it. Your unique voice, lived experience, expertise, imagination, and connections to your actual or potential audience are all available when you're ready to call upon them. And if you're reading this book, there's at least one idea inside you that wants to be in the world.

The true mystery and gift are how mundane the magic of writing is. Minutes of writing sentences, applied over time, become drafts of manuscripts. Quick emails to friends become conversations that unlock new pathways or epiphanies. Many small edits transform okay sentences into the micro-masterpieces that you'll be proud of for a lifetime.

With what's inside you and what's in these pages, you have everything you need to go from idea to book. Yes, you. Yes, today. Stand tall and start finishing.

—Charlie Gilkey, July 2021

Writing, like any creative process, is at turns thrilling and frustrating. When you're in the groove, it's exhilarating. When you're in a slump, it's devastating. Sometimes your work sings. Sometimes it falls flat. You doubt yourself. You think you're a genius. And on and on it goes.

Like most writers I know, I've been trying to "figure out my writing process" for almost as long as I've been putting words to paper. After all, I have eleventy billion stories I want to tell and get out into the world, and I'm always looking for the silver bullet to help me get my books across the finish line more quickly without losing quality. How can I cut "unproductive time" out of my process? How can I be more efficient? Get more done faster?

I was looking for that silver bullet when I took a course called Write Better-Faster from Becca Syme. I had just turned in the final book of my sci-fi series, the Bulari Saga, after several intense months of revisions. I was thrilled with the book, but I was frustrated by how long the revision process had taken.

Becca promises to help you use *your strengths as a writer* to improve the speed and quality of your work. *Your personal strengths*. It's right there in bold letters on her website, yet somehow going in I was still convinced she could change me into a different type of writer. One who can write 5,000 words a day and not have to edit, one who could outline novels rather than stumble through them.

Instead, she tried to help me embrace the kind of writer I am—one who discovers stories and characters as she writes, and for whom long, polishing revisions are integral to the writing process. My heart sank when Becca told me, "It's always going to take you longer than you want to write a book, because the other option is cutting corners, and you won't be happy with that."

And she was right. I like to dig for gold, and each revision pass reveals more gold. Every cycle I take through a scene reveals more of its truth, and my absolute favorite part of writing is when I've dug deep enough in my revisions that the story finally comes to life.

Becca was trying to tell me something critical about my writing process—but I still felt like I should be doing things differently. Faster. Like other writers.

One of the first books I read when I sat down to begin researching this book seriously was *Flow: The Psychology of Optimal Experience* by Mihaly Csikszentmihalyi. In the book, Csikszentmihalyi examines research on what makes people get "in the flow," whether they're working on a factory line or practicing the piano.

Surely he'd have some good tips for helping me be more productive.

Only one problem.

Csikszentmihalyi defines flow as, "A state in which people are so involved in an activity that nothing else seems to matter; the experience is so enjoyable that people will continue to do it even at great cost, for the sheer sake of doing it."

Wait up. Enjoyment? Isn't flow about productivity? About getting things done quickly and efficiently?

I started thinking back to when I was happiest writing. I can sometimes lose myself in a scene during the first draft, but I love polishing up what is already working, trying to find the perfect way to describe an emotional interaction, dialing in on a conversation until it gives me chills. When I'm revising, I get to experience my favorite moments over and over until they're perfect—it's like my own private viewing of the story before anyone else in the world gets to read it.

It's an experience so enjoyable that I'll continue to do it even at great cost, for the sheer sake of doing it.

Revision is the part of the process where I get into the flow state.

It dawned on me that I'd spent those months finishing my book series having very good writing days and feeling resentful of them because I was letting outside expectations get in the way.

So what if I spent an extra thirty minutes making sure that final conversation between two characters was spot on? I'd loved every one of those thirty minutes.

In my obsession to find a writing process that worked for me, I had been focused on the outcome. But what Becca Syme was trying to tell me—and what Mihaly Csikszentmihalyi was trying to tell me—is that it's actually about enjoying the process.

In my productivity guide, *From Chaos to Creativity: Building a Productivity System for Artists and Writers*, the goal was to help people build a process that works with their strengths to help them make time for their art. In this book, my goal is to help you take the best advantage of that writing time, by creating a writing process that brings you joy.

My hope is that by bringing you joy, your writing process will be the most productive one for you, personally.

If you're a writer, you're going to spend countless hours *writing*. Letting go of the outcomes and focusing on the act of writing itself results in better work and a higher probability that you'll achieve the outcome you want. Letting go of expectations about what it means to be a "real writer" lets you come up with a writing process that's enjoyable (and therefore more productive) to you.

What qualifies as "enjoyable and productive" will be unique to your writing process. Some writers try to hit a minimum word count. Others write for a set amount of time. Author Karen Russell said in a 2013 interview with the *Daily Beast* that she measures her own productivity in terms of the time she spent focused and immersed in her work. "Showing up and staying present is a good writing day," she said.[1]

As Anne Lamott writes in her memoir on writing, *Bird by Bird: Some Instructions on Writing and Life*, being a writer is often frustrating, and the path to publication is full of disappointments. You may start writing because you desire the outcome of a finished book, only to realize that writing is the best part.

1 "Karen Russell: How I Write." *Daily Beast*. February 6, 2013. https://www.thedailybeast.com/articles/2013/02/06/karen-russell-how-i-write.html

"It's like discovering that while you thought you needed the tea ceremony for the caffeine, what you really needed was the tea ceremony," she writes. "The act of writing turns out to be its own reward."

After all, if being a writer is fundamentally about the act of sitting down to write, why not make that act as enjoyable—and joyful—as possible?

Who Is This Book For?

Maybe you picked up this book because you have a story in you that you want to learn how to tell. Maybe you've been writing for a while, and you want to figure out how to have more of the good writing days. Maybe you're hoping I'll provide you with a silver bullet that will make your writing process smooth sailing from here on out and help you land a million-dollar contract.

(Spoiler alert: turns out I don't believe in silver bullets.)

Maybe you're feeling stuck in your process and looking for some new ideas to experiment with. Or maybe, like me, you've been resentful of your own process and think that you should somehow be a different kind of writer.

Maybe you want to hit the bestseller lists, or maybe you simply enjoy writing as a hobby—if you're writing, you're a writer.

Whatever spark drove you to pick up this book, my goal is to help you stop worrying about being the "right" kind of writer, and find a writing process that works best for you.

About This Book

In this book, you'll find the following parts.

We start, of course, with **planning**. How do you go from an unformed notion to a semi-coherent idea that's ready for you to start writing it? (Note that in this section I address outlining both for nonfiction and fiction writers, but whatever your cup of tea you'll find value in reading both!)

Then, we'll talk about **drafting**, the process of getting that idea on paper—both the logistics of starting the draft and how to keep yourself going through the tough parts.

When you have a final draft, it's time for **revising**, the process of making your draft into something coherent and shareable. We'll also touch on what to do once you're finished.

I broke these phases apart, but I don't want to imply there are hard lines between each. You may find it easiest to write the first draft if you have a detailed outline, extensive notes, and all your research at hand. Or you may find, like me, that drafting is part of your discovery process. In that case, you may cycle back to planning stage activities while you're drafting—or skip ahead to the draft in the planning stage to help you understand the shape of the project.

Similarly, you may be the sort of writer who wants everything out in a first draft before you go back and read anything you've written. Or you may cycle regularly between drafting and revising, reading through the words you wrote the day before or, like me, pausing whenever I get stuck in a draft to circle back and revise the section that came before so I have a solid footing to move forward with.

Finally, I'll discuss **what's next**, after you've finished the writing process, and I've included helpful **resources** in the form of books and podcasts.

I have pulled from my own experience writing fiction and nonfiction of all shapes and sizes, as well as interviews with other writers whose processes are quite different from my own. I also dip into some of my favorite books on writing and creativity for their wisdom.

Along the way, you'll find writing exercises and questionnaires to help you hone your process. The goal is to give you the tools to get started experimenting with a writing process that works best for you.

Let's do this.

Take Action

Think back through your own writing process and freewrite about it. Here are a few questions to help guide you:

- What's your favorite part of the writing process?

- When do you most often find yourself in the flow?

- What bumps you out of that flow?

- Where do you feel frustrated most frequently?

- What unconscious beliefs do you have about how "real writers" do things?

- How do those beliefs conflict with your natural writing process?

PART ONE

PLANNING

"Without leaps of imagination, or dreaming, we lose the excitement of possibilities. Dreaming, after all, is a form of planning." —Gloria Steinem

I once traveled with my dad to New York City for a writing conference, before smartphones. I booked us a room at a hostel north of downtown (yay, planning!), but I'd failed to write the address anywhere. We took the subway from the airport to downtown and, after struggling to find anywhere with free Wi-Fi to reassure my dad I knew where we were going, I finally declared that I basically knew where the hostel was. In my memory it was close to a subway stop—103rd Street sounded right—and if we got off there we'd be able to see the sign.

I didn't have the address, but I trusted my gut.

I was right.

We checked into the hostel, dumped our bags on the beds, and my dad turned to me and said, "Is this always how you travel? I'm so glad I didn't know this when you were backpacking around Europe and Venezuela. It would have given me a heart attack."

You probably already know if you're a detailed planner or a "by the seat of your pants" person by whether that story had you biting your nails or nodding your head like, "I've been there."

Every author plans—but the extent to which they plan differs. Writing a book is like building a cabin. Some authors like to have a detailed blueprint and all the wood cut and measured and ready to assemble before they hammer the first nail. Others start with a crayon sketch of a cabin, then set out into the woods to figure out which trees will work for lumber and let the building take shape as they go.

Both are planning in the way that works best for them.

For nonfiction, I tend to spend much more time researching and outlining, trusting that if I write a detailed outline, the project will stick to it. With fiction, I tend not to do much world-building or character development before I start drafting, trusting that it will work its way from my subconscious as I go. For that reason, with fiction I tend to cycle back and forth between the drafting and the planning stage until I get my bearings and can finish out the draft with confidence. (Of course, sometimes that doesn't happen until the climax of the book.)

I did very little up-front planning with my first sci-fi series, the Bulari Saga, and instead essentially felt my way through a five-book story arc. It was terrifying and made writing those last two books incredibly hard because the first three were published, and I still wasn't sure where I was going with the story.

I'm front-loading the planning a lot more for my next series. It's set in the same universe as the Bulari Saga, which means I'll have fewer unknowns concerning world-building. I'm also doing much more detailed work on characters and outlining before I dive into writing, in hopes that the drafting process will feel less out of control.

Will that work? Ask me next year. After all, I'm still the type of traveler who assumes things will turn out fine if I wing it. Smartphones have made doing this much easier than in the past, but I still love the thrill of arriving in a foreign city with a backpack and figuring out where we'll end up staying—even if it means not finding an affordable room and sleeping on the beach in San Sebastián while you and your girlfriend take turns keeping an eye out for creepers. Sorry Mom and Dad.

(Oh, fun fact: Dad and I missed our flight at the end of the trip because I remembered the day wrong, so don't be *too* impressed with the fact that I found that hostel.)

Planning Is Writing

One of the reasons many writers (*raises hand*) rush through the planning stage is that it doesn't feel like *writing*. I think that's partly because word count has become the most common measure of how productive a writing session is, and planning doesn't increase your word count.

Don't get me wrong. Your novel or article or blog post or memoir will absolutely not get written if you don't, you know, *write it*. But in a world where word count is the most visible metric of how productive your writing day was, don't forget about all the other parts of the writing process!

Charlie Gilkey, founder of Productive Flourishing and author of the award-winning book, *Start Finishing: How to Go from Idea to Done*, put it best. When I asked him what his favorite part of the writing process was, he said it was ideation.

"So much of the writing process doesn't look anything like writing," said Charlie. "It looks like reading. It looks like staring out the window. It looks like going on walks. For me, actually typing is at most 20 percent, the tip of the iceberg in terms of everything that happens in the writing process."

Don't feel a need to rush through the planning process to get to the drafting stage just because it feels more productive. Planning is all about coming to the blank page with a sketch, your materials, and your tool kit at the ready so that you can tackle your draft more effectively.

But on the flip side, don't feel like you need to drag your feet doing character bios or research just because you've been told you should do more planning. Some writers need more to get started, while others find that drafting is a critical part of discovering what they're writing about.

As I'll be saying over and over in this book, you do you.

A Couple of Notes

First, a caution. While prep work is important, don't let yourself get stuck there. Audience, goal, motivation—these are all things your book will need. But some of them may not become clear until you've done some writing. You can circle back, but don't let prep work become procrastination. At some point it's time to knuckle down and write.

Second, a lot of this work can be really helpful at the revision stage, too. So if you're reading this and worrying that you didn't do prep work before you started writing your current draft, no worries. It'll still be helpful. And if you haven't started writing yet and feel like you're stalling out on some of the following sections, don't sweat it. Maybe you need to skip ahead and start writing before you have a better sense of your idea, audience, theme, etc.

Third, are you looking for a deeper dive into how to effectively plan out creative work? I go into more depth in *From Chaos to Creativity*.

Take Action

People love to divide writers into two categories: planners (or plotters—more on that later) and "pantsers," who tell the story by the seat of their pants. What kind of writer are you—a planner or a fly-by-the-seat-of-your-pantser? Do some freewriting to help suss out your writing style. Ask yourself:

- Do you feel excited or intimidated by the idea of the blank page?

- What does ideation look like to you? Daydreaming? Freewriting? Talking with a friend?

- At what point in the planning process do you start champing at the bit to move on to drafting? Why then?

- If you're more of a planner, what do you admire about pantsers? And vice versa—if you prefer to pants your drafts, what do you admire about planners?

Now, let's dig into the planning process and talk about the strategies that work for both hardcore planners and free-spirited pantsers.

COMING UP WITH IDEAS

F rom a ten-book epic fantasy series to a haiku, every book, blog post, poem, and song starts with a spark of an idea.

A popular notion of a writer is that they sit down at the keyboard waiting for the muse to whisper in their ear. But in my experience the muse doesn't show up with a great idea unless you keep it well-fed with good creative inputs and give it plenty of time to process in the background. Only then will your muse become a reliable source for putting out ideas.

I got the idea of input, processing, and output from a fantastic short book called *Endless Ideas: Master Bottomless Creativity*, by Neeve Silver and Sean Platt. Silver and Platt envision idea generation as coming from a well-honed idea-making machine rather than my fuzzier, well-fed muse, and I highly recommend the book for their different strategies for collecting and processing ideas to work with.

You'll need ideas to get started writing, and you'll need ideas to keep feeding your work along the way. Whether you're writing fiction, nonfiction, memoir, or poetry one of the most valuable skills you can cultivate as part of your writing process is ideation: actively seeking and cultivating ideas.

Here are some things to try whether you're a planner or a pantser.

Get Inspired

Writers—and all artists—take inspiration from everything around them. As Austin Kleon writes in *Steal Like an Artist: 10 Things Nobody Told You about Being Creative*, "Every new idea is just a mash-up or remix of one or more previous ideas." He points out that when you search for ideas in the works of authors you admire, you get more than fodder for your muse. You also get a crash course in how that author sees the world—which can help hone your own way of seeing the world.

Search for inspiration from writers you admire, but also look at things outside your field. You can find sparks of ideas in other art, of course, but also in things that seem completely unrelated to what you're working on. Why not pick up a farm implement catalog and peruse that? Read an interview with a long-distance runner. Take a class on CAD design or Swedish cooking.

Get Bored

Sometimes the best ideas come when you completely zone out and let your mind wander. These days, our minds are used to being constantly entertained. We've got a movie on in the background, a podcast in the car, the radio playing in the shower, our phone in our hand in the checkout line. And as Manoush Zomorodi points out in her book *Bored and Brilliant: How Spacing Out Can Unlock Your Most Productive and Creative Self*, all this distraction gets in the way of our creativity.

She offers a series of challenges to wean you off distraction like, "no looking at your phone while you're in transit from one location to the next." I highly recommend reading the book and putting some of the practices into place.

Then just . . . let yourself get bored and see what bubbles up.

I go on a lot of walks around our neighborhood. I used to make them "productive" by always listening to a podcast or dictating a draft of something as I walked. But more and more I'm using them as a time to let my brain wander unfettered. Though I sometimes have a specific problem to think about (like how on earth will I end my novel!?!?), going for a walk and checking in with myself about how I'm doing always leaves me feeling refreshed.

I don't always come home with a brilliant insight, but I definitely feel calmer, and my muse is able to work along in the background.

Get Distracted

The MacGyver Secret: Connect to Your Inner MacGyver and Solve Anything by Lee David Zlotoff (MacGyver's creator) and Colleen Seifert, PhD, offers a more deliberate take on the idea of getting bored. After he noticed he got his best ideas in the shower or while running mindless errands, Zlotoff started turning that common experience into something he could tap into at will.

Eventually, he settled on a simple-yet-effective process. When he's stuck, he simply jots the question he needs answered on his office whiteboard. Then, rather than banging his head against his computer trying to come up with an answer (like I tend to do), Zlotoff sits down and works on model building kits.

And he doesn't think about the question. At all.

After an hour or so of letting his subconscious mull things over, Zlotoff heads back to his whiteboard and starts brainstorming.

(The process is slightly more complicated, and *The MacGyver Secret* is definitely worth a read.)

The idea is that whatever mindless yet repetitive activity you've chosen (a shower, a hike, a bike ride, working in the garden, building a model), it occupies what Zlotoff calls "that endless hamster wheel of spinning thoughts" in your head so your subconscious can work on the question you asked. And believe me—your subconscious can be incredibly creative if you're not yelling at it to come up with ideas! This is one of my new favorite ways of ideation.

Scratch Out Small Ideas

Choreographer Twyla Tharp, in her excellent book *The Creative Habit: Learn It and Use It for Life*, talks about "scratching" for inspiration. When she scratches for ideas, she's not hoping to be hit by a thunderbolt of inspiration—she's out exploring with an open mind, curious. She might "scratch" by doing something dance-adjacent, like listening to music or attending another choreographer's performance. Or she might be reading a magazine and make a sudden connection between something completely unrelated to dance and her current project.

Tharp's process of scratching may not be formalized, but she does take care to keep her mind open and capture these flashes of insight as they come.

She writes that big ideas seldom come on their own. "That is why you scratch for little ideas. Without the little ideas, there are no big ideas."

In his delightful book of essays, *Zen in the Art of Writing*, science fiction author Ray Bradbury likens this search for ideas to dropping stones down a well. "Every time you hear an echo from your subconscious, you know yourself a little better. A small echo may start an idea. A big echo may result in a story."

Start Brainstorming

Soaking up ideas in your daily life is lovely, but brainstorming exercises can be helpful if you're looking for something specific—a villain's backstory, a compelling blog topic, a better way to describe an emotional beat in a poem.

Here are some brainstorming techniques to try. (The first two are tips I got from *Endless Ideas*.)

- The 50 Things List: Frame the problem you're trying to solve in a positive light (e.g., "Here are some of the topics my audience loves reading about"). Then set a timer for fifteen minutes and come up with fifty ideas. Just keep writing ideas without judgement.

- An Idea a Day: Start a list, and add one thing to it every day. I used this method when I was starting to plan my Nanshe

Chronicles series, an episodic heist-type series that would need lots of unique situations, settings, and characters. For months, I jotted down one potential story idea a day, and that list has become the backbone of my brainstorming now that I'm plotting the series.

- Mind Map: Grab a sheet of paper or open up a mind-mapping app (I like Scapple), and let your brain start to come up with connections between things. I find this method is fantastic for nonfiction, whether planning out a book or brainstorming blog post ideas.

List What Thrills You

In *Zen in the Art of Writing*, Bradbury writes about how he learned to come up with ideas that were truly his. He had spent years imitating the popular science fiction and detective writers of the time, paying attention to what stories sold to magazines and trying to come up with similar ideas—only to have them fall flat.

Eventually, he began to write lists of fears and loves, digging back through his psyche and memories to find the things that had truly terrified or thrilled him. The dark ravine behind his childhood home. The carnival. The mirror maze. The town clock. The carousel.

He began to run through those lists, picking a noun and freewriting until it sparked into something that resonated with him.

Paying attention to what thrilled, delighted, and terrified him as he wrote is what led to such immersive, weird, and gorgeously haunting stories like *Dandelion Wine* and *Something Wicked This Way Comes*.

Jennifer Lynn Barnes, PhD, a young adult author and expert on the psychology of fiction, has spoken at conferences like Romance Writers of America and on podcasts such as *Red Sneaker Writers*[2] about keeping an "Id List" of the tropes, characters, and details that are irresistible to you as a reader, then using those to inspire you. For her, that list is hundreds of items long, including everything from twins to scenes set on rooftops.

Don't worry about what's popular, whether space dragons are currently hot, or if self-help books for moms seem to be selling well. Start creating your own lists of nouns, phrases, and tropes you find magnetic, and trust others will love them in your own work.

Ideas are a dime a dozen, and generic ideas are even cheaper. But when you pay attention to what thrills and amazes *you*, you'll transform these generic ideas into something truly unique.

Keeping Track of Your Ideas

In the idea-generation stage, it may end up being days—or even years—before you start work. Or you may have one project percolating in the background while you're working on something else. How do you keep track of all these ideas?

2 "Using the Id List to Enhance Fiction." *Red Sneaker Writers*. December 17, 2018. spreaker.com/user/willbern/008-interview-with-jennifer-lynn-barnes

By nurturing them in an idea garden until you're ready to use them.

Science fiction and fantasy author Fonda Lee has a file folder of ideas that she revisits every so often. "I tend to sit with ideas for a long time," she told me in an interview. "I have this drawer of ideas that I'm always pruning and adding to, but the ones that I end up working on are the ideas where a year or two has gone by, and I still think it's a good idea."

For a long time, I kept everything in a series of college-ruled spiral-bound notebooks. Each one would last me two to five months, and when I was done, I'd go back through and highlight any story ideas or thoughts I wanted to keep an eye on, tagging the pages with little colored sticky note flags so I could find things more easily.

Now I use Evernote, in part because I wanted to digitize my process since I was always traveling, and in part because writing longhand was upsetting my wrist. I have different notebooks for different projects, which I group as In Progress, Simmering, Finished, or Parked.

When I have an idea, whether it's for a current project or a "someday" project, I can drop it in the right notebook and then, when I'm ready to work on that project, all my ideas are in one spot.

Once I'm ready to start working, I transfer my notes and such to Scrivener (a word processing software), and any new ideas get placed right in the Scrivener file for that project.

Take Action

Start thinking of idea generation as a part of your writing process, and turn it into a habit. Create an idea garden (whether that's a file folder, a separate notebook, a note on your phone, or a shoebox), then begin regularly adding ideas to that garden using some of the methods in this section.

- Reread one of your favorite writer's works, and list the things you love: snippets of prose, word choice, themes, literary devices, etc.

- Spend an afternoon bored. Leave your phone at home (or on airplane mode), and go for a walk with no destination, or simply stare out the window of the bus on your commute rather than bringing a book. Then, jot down the places your mind wandered to.

- Try the MacGyver Secret to let your subconscious do the work while you're distracting your chattering brain.

- Collect fragments of ideas that thrill you, and then "scratch" at them by freewriting until something surfaces.

- Use one of the brainstorming techniques above to come up with a list of new ideas.

DEVELOPING YOUR IDEA

N ow that you have an interesting idea (or ten) to write about, how do you go about turning it from a dim spark of inspiration into something that can stand on its own two feet?

As I've thought about my own process and studied the processes of others, I've broken idea development down into four broad steps. Of course, depending on your idea, the lines between each of these steps might be blurry, or individual steps may be unnecessary.

Step 1: Find the Spark and Improvise on It

Start by asking yourself what you find fascinating about the idea. What's causing it to ping about in your subconscious? When you understand why you're interested, you're one step closer to presenting it in a way that makes others perk up their ears.

Freewriting is one of the best tools a writer has at their disposal for idea generation and development. Through freewriting, you can mine your subconscious for the things that are tugging for your attention, surfacing memories, observations, and turns of phrase that are begging to become something more.

It's also one of the best ways to start synthesizing your small ideas into a big one. In fact, it's the main technique that works for me. I may have an idea for a character, a vague situation, a snippet of dialogue, a hint of a theme—but until I sit down and start writing, those won't coalesce into anything more than disparate parts.

For Twyla Tharp, improvisational movement is her form of freewriting. "[Improvisation] is your one opportunity in life to be completely free, with no responsibilities and no consequences," Tharp writes in *The Creative Habit*. "You don't have to be good or great or even interesting. It's you alone, with no one watching or judging. If anything comes of it, you decide whether the world gets to see it."

Improvising doesn't have to mean freewriting—you could tease out your idea through daydreaming or a conversation with a friend.

Step 2: Define the Core and Feel Out the Edges
When you have a strong sense of what fascinates you about an idea, start feeling out its shape.

A strong idea will have a core (you might also call this a theme or central question), which will keep you focused as you write.

In the case of nonfiction, this is often literally a question you want your readers to have an answer to by the end of the book. ("How can I have a better relationship with my spouse?" "Where are the best hikes in the Puget Sound?")

With fiction, the seed of your story might be a character, a world-building element, or a plot point. You might have a fun mash-up idea (*"Pacific Rim* but about opera singers"; *"The Da Vinci Code* but with space pirates"), or you may have a vague sense of a character and situation, like I did for my first published novel. ("An overworked mother of three agrees to help her estranged sister resurrect the ghost of her dead lover and ends up accidentally possessed.")

Your job is to take that seed and turn it into a core idea to shape your story around. To take my first novel as an example, the seed of a character and situation turned into the core idea: "When we protect ourselves from grief and loss, we risk pushing away our loved ones while they're still alive." That core idea shaped the plot, and the main character's relationships with her sister, her children, and the ghost she ends up hosting.

Twyla Tharp calls this core idea the spine and defines it as "the statement you make to yourself outlining your intentions for the work." For Tharp, spine isn't something the audience ever needs to see; it's there solely to keep you on track as you're creating.

"You will still get lost on occasion," she writes, "but having a spine will anchor you. When you lose your way, it will show you the way home. It will remind you that this is what you have set out to do, this is the story you're trying to tell, this is the effect you're trying to achieve."

Along with defining the core of your idea, you also need to feel out the edges. Are you writing an epic saga? An intimate family drama? A short series of blog posts? A book-length manifesto? (We'll talk more about finding the size of your project soon.)

In *Die Empty: Unleash Your Best Work Every Day*, Todd Henry calls this "setting parameters for your problem," and likens it to starting with the edge pieces of a jigsaw puzzle. Once you can see the edges of the problem you're solving, it keeps you focused on doing relevant work, whether that's research or developing characters.

"When you have clear boundaries to work within," he writes, "you feel more comfortable asking extremely diverse questions and exploring initially irrelevant-seeming possibilities. Structure and freedom are two sides of the same coin. Structure yields freedom to creatively roam."

When doing this work, try to keep things as simple as possible. The simpler the question, the more powerful your writing will be.

Step 3: Write Out Your Idea Succinctly

As someone who writes fiction basically by super gluing my hands to the tail of a distracted yellow lab and holding on for dear life while it runs on an adventure, the idea of knowing what you're trying to say ahead of time is foreign to me.

So when I heard suspense author J.D. Barker on an episode of *The Creative Penn* podcast[3] say that he writes the back cover copy

3 "How to Develop Bestselling Story Ideas with J.D. Barker." *The Creative Penn.* June 22, 2020. thecreativepenn.com/2020/06/22/bestselling-story-ideas/

for his novels before he starts writing the draft, I was stunned. Especially since he, like me, doesn't really outline his books.

How on earth can he know where he's going before he starts?

Barker worked for years as a book doctor before he started writing his own novels, so he has a very strong sense of what a story should be—especially a commercially viable story. He uses the blurb as a tool, the North Star of his story, and he reads it every day before he starts writing to make sure he's always headed in that direction.

I decided to give this a shot as I began plotting out the first books in my space pirates series. After all, I know what ideas and phrases get my spine tingling and make me press the buy button when I read a good book blurb. And writing that out for my own books ahead of time is helping me stay focused on telling that story and weeding through anything extraneous.

For nonfiction, I find it easier to write out the idea ahead of time than for fiction. Like, "This book will help you discover a writing process that's productive and enjoyable so you can succeed as a writer in the long-term." Or, "This book will help you nail your content marketing strategy and land more clients."

But sometimes it takes time to discover that North Star, and sometimes you realize you need to realign your compass as the idea develops in the draft. That's fine. I do recommend you take a stab at writing out your idea ahead of time, though.

And hey, if that sounds implausible to you, and you're just starting out writing your first project, maybe you need to take a few laps with the distracted yellow lab first. That's totally fine.

UNDERSTANDING YOUR AUDIENCE

When I turned in the last book of the Bulari Saga to my editor, I was terrified that everyone would hate how I ended the story arc. I have readers who are invested in the characters and story of the first four books of the series, and I was worried they'd have other opinions about what the main character should have done.I was explaining all this to my husband in anguish one night, and he asked a simple question.

"Do you think the ending is satisfying?"

"Yeah," I answered. "I love the ending so much."

He shrugged. "Then stop worrying about what other people will think."

Robert was right. Because, first and foremost, you're writing for yourself.

Maybe some readers will be turned off by the ending. Maybe I'll get complaints. But in the end, I'm writing books I want to read. I'm my first target reader, and if I don't love the story I'm telling, how could I expect anyone else to?

In *Zen in the Art of Writing*, Bradbury tells a story illustrating this idea that I find both heartbreaking and absolutely charming. When he was nine years old, he collected Buck Rogers comic strips. His friends made fun of him so relentlessly that he finally tore up the strips.

"For a month I walked through my fourth-grade classes, stunned and empty," he writes. "One day I burst into tears, wondering what devastation had happened to me. The answer was: Buck Rogers. He was gone, and life simply wasn't worth living. The next thought was: those are not my friends, the ones who got me to tear the strips apart and so tear my own life down the middle; they are my enemies."

Bradbury went back to collecting Buck Rogers, he writes, and was happy from then on. "For that was the beginning of my writing science fiction. Since then, I have never listened to anyone who criticized my taste in space travel, sideshows, or gorillas. When this occurs, I pack up my dinosaurs and leave the room."

Yes, you need to think about your audience if you want your writing to reach them in a meaningful way. But your interests, your passion, your voice needs to drive your work, not theirs.

If someone else is trying to shape the story you're trying to tell?

Pack up your dinosaurs and leave the room.

Defining Your Audience

That said, unless you're journaling, other people will eventually read your work. And if you want to delight, entertain, serve, and inspire them, you need to know your audience.

In my day job, I'm a freelance content marketing writer for B2B companies and thought leaders. One of the first things most of my clients will do is send me their buyer personas, which are fictionalized people who represent their target market. Having these buyer personas is immensely helpful for me when I'm writing marketing copy, because instead of thinking, "Surely all Chief Technical Officers would like a better solution for security training," I can imagine Maria, "a forty-three-year-old mother of three who's CTO of CoolStartupX, just wants to get home for her daughter's recital, but first she has to deal with that phishing scam in the HR department. You know what would make her damn day? An on-budget way to automate security training."

Then, because I have a strong idea of what Maria's problems, goals, and dreams are, I can write copy that's compelling for her specifically—and actually reads as more appealing to a broader audience. If I was just trying to write to a group of faceless CTOs, my copy would end up feeling generic and, ironically, appeal to no one at all.

It may sound counterintuitive to think of one single person as you're writing— don't you want to reach as wide an audience as possible? The problem is that when you try to write something that appeals to everyone, your message feels bland and watered down. Having an ideal reader in mind helps keep you focused on writing a book, article, or short story that has specific appeal. It answers your reader's questions, tugs at their heartstrings, plucks at their imagination, solves their problems.

If you're writing fiction, you may be writing to a modern-day teenage version of yourself, who just wants to read every fantasy novel with a kickass queer sword-wielding protagonist she can get her hands on. Call her Shandra. As you're writing this "learning to wield her superpower" scene or that "butch swordswoman meets the princess she's supposed to guard for the first time" scene, let yourself imagine Shandra's reaction.

If you're writing nonfiction, you may picture a harried, thirty-two-year-old modern professional office worker who wants to quit work and follow their passions. Let's call them Jace. Is that line about "opening your heart to possibilities" going to strike Jace as too cheesy? Is Jace going to pump their fist at the success stories you're including in the book? What other questions might Jace have that you haven't thought to answer?

You may even have a flesh-and-blood person in mind. Novelist Stephen King famously writes for his wife Tabitha. She's the person whose opinion of his work matters the most. In *On Writing: A Memoir of the Craft*, King writes that every novelist has a single ideal reader and notes they'll be in your writing room all the time, "in the flesh once you open the door and let the world back in to shine on the bubble of your dream, in spirit during the sometimes troubling and often exhilarating days of the first draft, when the door is closed."

I have a few early readers that I keep in mind as I write. I will write scenes and think, Andrea's gonna love that. Or, Nathanael and Tara are definitely going to text me about that! Or, Tina's gonna get a kick out of it when this character walks on screen.

My husband Robert isn't necessarily my ideal reader, but he is my first reader—so when he gives me feedback I have to filter it through the lens of my target audience. He actually didn't like the ending of the Bulari Saga. We went around and around as he tried to convince me to try something different, but I felt passionately that my ending was the right one. Arguing with him about it forced me to articulate why but also gave me a chance to address the aspects of my ending that he was bouncing off of. The result was that my risky ending was made much stronger— and more appealing to my ideal reader because I leaned in harder to what was important while paring away what was distracting.

So keep your ideal reader in mind as you're planning your book— but remember that they come second to you when it comes to actually writing your draft.

Take Action

Use the following questions to define your ideal reader:

Nonfiction

- Demographics: Age, gender, race, religion, etc. (if applicable)

- What is the biggest problem they're trying to solve, and why?

- What are their dreams? Hobbies? Passions? Fears? Worries?

- What do they hope reading your book will do for them?

- What other books have they read on this topic?

- What's their reading style like? Do they read in short bursts on the go, or do they have time to curl up for hours and learn?

Fiction

- Demographics: Age, gender, race, religion, etc. (if applicable)

- What are some of their other favorite books and authors?

- What are their favorite tropes?

- What kinds of stories do they like to read?

- Why do they like to read? To be entertained? To explore new worlds? To solve puzzles? To meet interesting new people?

- How many books a month do they normally read?

Now that you know what you're writing about and who your ideal reader is, let's talk about research. The amount of research you do before you get started writing will vary depending on your project, genre, and writing style. You may not need to research much if you're writing a memoir or a contemporary novel set somewhere you're familiar with. Or you may spend years researching if you're writing something more involved.

Nonfiction

Adonia E. Lugo, PhD, author of *Bicycle/Race: Transportation, Culture, & Resistance*, comes from an academic background with a heavy emphasis on research.

"What I really enjoy about doing research is having a sense of following a trail," she told me. "It's like trying to sense your way through how this topic is connected to that topic."

When we spoke, her latest project, a historical piece tied to a distant relative, had her spending a lot of time in online archives and visiting places around Los Angeles to study certain aspects of the city's built environment. She uses spreadsheets and the reference management software Zotero to track the books and articles she reads, as well as her field notes and other anecdotes.

For Adonia, the research process tends to blend with the drafting process, as she finds inspiration in her research and starts wrestling with ideas. "Sometimes it's tough for me to know where the research ends and the trying to craft together a narrative begins," she said. "And I think even having that distinction is something I need to get rid of, because I find it really productive to be doing research. Maybe I need to let go of the idea that there's a research phase and then there's a writing phase, and let them continue to happen together."

The nonfiction research phase is where you inform yourself, but it's also where you hone your idea by exploring what else has been written about the topic so you can write your own work in conversation with other writers.

When I write nonfiction, I start by surveying everything that's out there on the topic. For this project, for example, I scoured my own bookshelves and quizzed other writers on their favorite writing process books. I then sat down over the course of a few months and read through the massive stack, taking notes as I went and writing bits of chapters and anecdotes as they came to mind. Finally, I turned to the interview stage of research, which is my favorite because I feel that's where you find the most unique information.

With each book I read and interview I completed, I grouped the most interesting quotes and concepts under bigger headings like Drafting and Research. When I was finished with the last interview, I could then look back through all my sketched-out chapters and see where I needed to go searching for more material.

One note: When you're gathering research and talking to interview subjects, pay attention to whose voices you're listening to. Because the definition of who got to be an expert was limited to cis white men for millennia, if you just seek out the "top voices" you might end up with a sample of ideas that is skewed toward that demographic. Dig a bit deeper to find authors and experts who represent as wide a range of life experiences as possible, and your own work will have more depth and be more relevant to your audience.

Fiction

When it comes to fiction, I know writers who will dive in and research on an as-needed basis (*raises hand*) and others who will audit entire college courses to learn what they need to start writing.

Science fiction author Curtis C. Chen told me the amount of research he does before diving into writing the first draft depends on how much the story hinges on a particular aspect. When writing a story set in a floating city on Venus, he did a ton of research first to nail down the basics of the science; for other stories, he does his research afterward in order to fill in the gaps and make his settings and technology more realistic.

When I went to a book launch party for Fonda Lee's *Zeroboxer*, I was blown away by the PowerPoint presentation she gave about her research process for coming up with the aliens. As a writer who just makes up details until someone says they're implausible, I knew I needed to ask her more about her research process.

Fonda told me she breaks research into two categories: exploratory prewriting research and tactical research done during writing or revision to home in on details.

Before she starts writing, she usually spends two or three months in the exploratory prewriting research phase, reading what interests her and learning about the things she wants to include in the story. For her Green Bone Saga, she started with the aesthetic idea for the world, rather than characters or plot, then she filled a notebook with things she wanted to research in order to build on that kernel of an idea, including wuxia fiction, kung fu films, gangster flicks, the rise of Asian economies in the twentieth century, jade mining, and drug cartels in Mexico.

Fonda normally reads with a physical notebook at her side to jot down cool stuff, and after she's spent some time learning and reading, she'll begin organizing her notes for actual use with Evernote and Scrivener. She uses folders like "world-building," "weapons," "names," etc. and starts dropping research into the appropriate folder.

Eventually she'll start transforming that real-world research into story magic by freewriting about the history of the world, how religion works, and everything else she needs to know.

In the pre-research stage, she'll often learn things that will give her whole plot points, she told me. For example, when she was researching for *Zeroboxer*, digging into current laws around genetic engineering led her to make the legal consequences of genetic engineering pertinent to the plot.

"That's the sort of thing where I might have a vague general story idea," she said. "But it's in that prewriting research that the actual meat of the world and the story come into focus."

Joanna Penn, host of the amazing writing podcast *The Creative Penn*, is another author whose research fundamentally shapes her novels. She writes thriller novels, as J.F. Penn, that are based in the real world and informed by her own love of travel, so she's always on the lookout for interesting historical connections—visiting cathedrals, museums, art galleries, and anywhere else that has history and art and culture to spark story ideas.

The process is extremely organic, Joanna told me. For example the spark of her novel *Valley of Dry Bones* came when she visited the cathedral in Palma de Mallorca and saw a statue of a friar who founded missions on the West Coast of the United States. Later travels to San Francisco and New Orleans unearthed other connections to the friar and to the Spanish Inquisition, and inspired a trip to Toledo, Spain, to hunt for more information.

"It's a snowball effect," she told me. "One little bit of an idea turns into more research, which turns into more ideas until I know I've got enough to write a novel."

She doesn't take many notes but instead takes lots of pictures and buys books on local history wherever she goes. "What happens in my brain is this idea of synchronicity that fits together over time," she said. Once she feels that she has enough for a story, she starts organizing things in Scrivener and knitting together the book.

Whether or not you're making up a world out of whole cloth, doing your research ahead of time gives you a good foundation to start from. Or, you may prefer to dive in and explore the world as you go.

Either way, only you know how much research you need to feel comfortable telling the story you want.

Knowing When to Stop Research

Whether you're writing nonfiction or fiction, there's a real danger of getting caught in the research phase and not moving on to the actual work of writing. I know authors who have spent years creating religions and languages for fantasy novels they've barely written a few thousand words of.

And you know what? That's totally fine if your happy place is world-building and you don't care about finishing a draft. Like I said in the introduction, there's no one right way to be a writer, and it's perfectly fine to enjoy the writing process without wanting to be a bestseller or land an agent, or any of the other outcome-related goals generally associated with publishing your work.

But if you do want to publish that book someday, to avoid getting stuck in the research phase, go back to the work you did developing your idea. Let your core idea and project framework act as a yardstick against which you can measure what type and how much research you need to do.

Will reading Jon Lee Anderson's eight-hundred-page biography of Che Guevara inform the characters and plot of the space pirate series I'm working on? Yes. Should I put the entire project on hold until I finish reading that door stopper? No, because the project doesn't hinge on that research.

Research is a fun and fundamental part of the writing process, and only you know if you are actually working on your project, or if you're procrastinating on doing the actual work.

Take Action

As you're researching, keep everything in one place to make sure you don't lose any of your ideas.

For example, I have a folder in Evernote for the series I'm currently working on. Whenever I come across an interesting idea or article, I can jot it down on a note there, or even clip the entire article to the folder.

I take notes from any book I might be reading as research in Evernote, as well. I start a note in my series folder with the title and author, then use it to record facts, my thoughts, and memorable quotes. Sometimes this will spark my own brainstorming, which I then record in that same note.

Once I'm solidly in the drafting phase of the project, I start to tease out the most important bits of those notes and organize those in my Scrivener project. For a fiction project, I'll start sections on Politics, Characters, or History. For a nonfiction project, I'll start to collect research based on topics like Outlining, Drafting, or Revising.

Whether you prefer digital or physical, create a central place to house your research:

- Set up a physical file folder to collect paper notes.

- Start a new folder on your computer or in a notes app like Evernote, OneNote, or Notion to collect digital notes.

- Buy a fresh notebook (or pull one of the dozens of blank ones off your shelf—I see you!) to jot down your research.

A quick tip: As you dive in and start writing, keep a running list of things you need to look up. When you get the urge to jump out of your draft and Wikipedia something, add it to the list to look up later. This can help curb the tendency many writers have to procrastinate by researching.

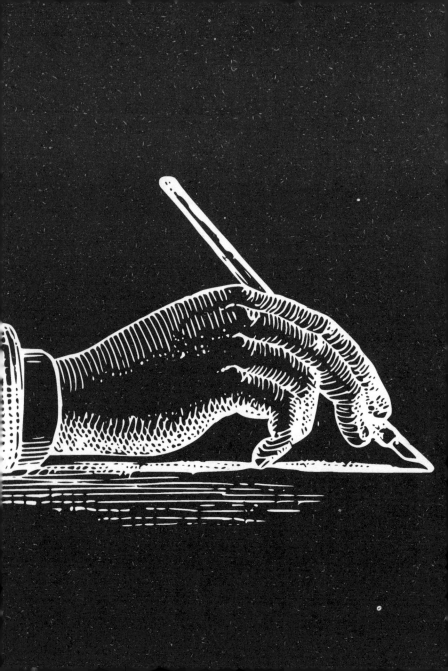

OUTLINING

Outlining nonfiction

At this stage, your book, zine, or article is dozens of half-formed ideas whirling across your attention like a dust devil. Your seemingly impossible job is to turn that dust devil into a finished product with a beginning, middle, and end.

If it feels impossible right now, don't worry.

Every time I sit down to write something new, turning that dust devil of ideas into a finished piece is daunting as hell. But when I remember that each book or article is simply a collection of chapters and subsections it feels easier.

As you sort through your research, notes, and thoughts, remember your most important tool: your core idea.

Maybe you've been finessing your core idea as you did your planning and prep work; maybe you threw it out entirely when you realized your research or passion was pointing you in the direction of a new core idea. Whatever the case, your core idea will guide you as you break down your topic into pieces and organize them into the most effective order.

Right now, you're trying to bridge the gap between having a solid idea to having a solid *story*. This is true for both fiction and nonfiction. Nonfiction may not have as many wild twists and turns as a thriller novel or an episode of *Breaking Bad*, but it still has a flow. Your self-help book or business guide still needs to lead the reader on a journey from introduction to conclusion.

Break Down Your Idea to Find the Story

The term "breaking the story" comes from screenwriting, and Vince Gilligan, writer and producer of the *X-Files* and creator of *Breaking Bad*, called breaking the story the most crucial part of the writing process in an interview with the Television Academy Foundation.[4] He described sitting in the writer's room with a cork board, a stack of 3x5 cards, and Sharpies and organizing the episode into a teaser and four acts. After that, he said, the writing is carefree because you've already done the hard work.

Breaking the story isn't just for fiction writers. Nonfiction books have a structure all their own, and understanding how yours is shaped will help you immensely when it comes to the drafting process.

Charlie Gilkey likens developing a nonfiction book to building a stone wall. He starts gathering the big stones—the major ideas, arguments, and research the book will be built on—then organizes them in the right sequence. As he works on this process, which can take three or four months, he may realize that he's missing a few stones and needs to go back to the quarry

4 "Interview: Vince Gilligan." *Television Academy Foundation*. September 9, 2011. interviews. televisionacademy.com/interviews/vince-gilligan

and do some research. Or rearrange some in order to build a stronger argument.

"Once I know they're stacked right, I can put some of the mortar in between them," he told me. "The fascia that makes it work."

Start by gathering the big stones of your idea—the major questions you have, the topics you know you want to cover, the arguments you definitely want to hit. (Note that when you're breaking your story, you're simultaneously jotting down everything you know and giving yourself permission to be curious about the things you don't know.) Once you can see the discrete bits of information that will make up your whole piece, you can start grouping them together.

Then, **go back to your core idea.**

This will help you start organizing your ideas as well as sifting through to find the ones that are most important, setting aside those that don't fit. It will also help you organize all the subtopics and sections you're brainstorming into the most effective argument.

When I started working on this book, I opened up a mind mapping tool and brainstormed everything I could about the topic, "How do you come up with a writing process that you'll enjoy?" Then I sat down with a couple of friends to brainstorm even more ideas, since this is a topic I'm really familiar with, and they had a bunch of interesting questions I wouldn't have thought to ask. That gave me an outline, a framework to begin organizing my research and interviews.

Sometimes, it helps to get analogue. I'll often take over one end of the dining table and break the story on 3x5 cards like Vince described. Once you have things grouped by topic, you'll start to see the order they should come in. For example, chapters about writing the book need to come before chapters about revising the book.

You may not have a clear path, but for now just try to see the shape of beginning, middle, and end.

Once I have a solid outline, I'll add all the individual sections into Scrivener so that I can tackle them one at a time. I write using Scrivener because it allows you to break a long document into subsections that are easy to move around and reorganize. (Other authors use tools like Ulysses and OneNote in the same way.)

For book-length projects, I set up individual folders within the draft for sections, then create sub-documents for each chapter within the section. This helps me see at a glance what I'm working on in the draft, and I jump around if I suddenly have an idea I want to add to the chapter on Getting Unstuck or need to check a fact back in the Introduction.

For articles, I don't create separate sub-documents for each section, but I do jot down a list of headings and notes under each heading so I can see the overall structure of the piece.

Remember. This step can take days or months or years as you gather research, or mine your childhood memories, or develop your thoughts on a topic. That's fine. This part of the writing process is just as critical as the drafting, and some writers will need to have a stronger organizational foundation than others in order to get started.

Take Action

Try a few different methods to find out what works best for you to break the story and get organized:

- Mind map with a whiteboard, paper, or app: jot down everything you know about a topic, and start to organize it into sections that link together.

- Use sticky notes or 3x5 cards to collect ideas for sections, then physically rearrange them until they make sense.

- Explain everything you know about your topic to a friend, and record the conversation. Then go through the transcription and highlight the different main ideas.

As you sort through your main ideas about your topic, take note of which ones excite you the most, and set aside the ones that don't seem to fit with your core idea. Once you have your ideas grouped in different subsections, try to understand the natural beginning, middle, and end, then put them in the order that makes the most sense to you.

Outlining Fiction

As I was writing the Bulari Saga, I cannot count the number of times I was tearing my hair out about not knowing what would happen next when Robert gently said, "Have you considered outlining? That might help."

My reply was an anguished wail followed by obscenities and a shot of whiskey.

I did have an outline.

But my story didn't pay any damn attention to my outlines.

Outlining nonfiction is fantastic. You come up with the major points, put them in order, and then write the damn thing. But fiction is a totally different beast. I'll regularly come up with a perfectly wonderful outline that hits all the storytelling beats and has a satisfying conclusion, and on page three my protagonist is like, "Thanks for the map to Minneapolis, but I lit it on fire and decided to hitchhike to Tucson. Peace out, loser."

I don't know if it sounds crazy when fiction writers say their characters make decisions without them, because I spend too much time with fiction writers, and most of us say that. When I was lamenting my inability to stick to an outline to my friend Mark Teppo, author of *Finish Your Novel!: A Writer Productivity Guide*, he laughed and said, "I had a great outline for this next book I'm writing, but my main character shot and killed the villain in the first chapter so now I have to redo my outline." He'd done enough thinking about the book ahead of time that he came up with a fix pretty easily, but it was still a pain.

Of course, other fiction writers (alas, not me!) have strong outlining chops. Grant Rosenberg, whose long career as a writer and producer gave us television shows like *Bitten*, *Lost Girl*, and *Lois & Clark: The New Adventures of Superman*, is one such writer. Most recently, Grant has turned to novels. When he was working on his first thriller, *Gideon*, he used the 3x5 card method to break the story of his novel, then wrote out a timeline to keep the four simultaneous stories of his thriller straight.

"I did a full outline on my novel before I wrote it," Grant told me. "It changed while I was writing it, but at least I had a map of where it was going." With television writing, Grant would use that blueprint to write all fifty-four pages of the script in one pass before going back and editing. With his novel, he did end up revising some of the beginning when he got a cool idea that put a wrench in the character's development, but otherwise the outline helped him to get the first draft of his novel out quickly.

Should you outline? Is outlining inherently better than not? As with all the advice in this book, the answer is, "It depends."

Earlier in the Planning section, you did some writing to discover whether you are more of a planner or a pantser. The truth is, most writers I know fall somewhere in the middle of the spectrum, taking tools from the workbenches of both plotters (in the case of writing fiction) and pantsers to come up with a process that works for them personally. And you'll also find that some projects will lend themselves more readily to the outlining approach. For example, while the Bulari Saga was a capricious beast of a rambling series, the series I'm working on now is modeled off the beats of episodic television shows, and sticking to an outline has been much easier.

Which method is better isn't the right question. A better question is, "What works best for me?" What tools can you use to get you through your first draft with the maximum amount of productivity and—most importantly—enjoyment?

Keep experimenting with the amount of outlining you do and the amount of freedom you give yourself to make things up on the fly. The more you write, the more you'll learn what works best for you, and what approach will be the best for a particular project.

Let's take a look at both ends of the spectrum.

Pantsing

I love the way sci-fi and western writer Dean Wesley Smith talks about finding a story in his book, *Writing into the Dark: How to Write a Novel without an Outline*. Smith describes writing fiction as being an explorer with a dim flashlight, trying to make your way through a complicated cave system. You may head down the wrong path sometimes, but you just find your way back to the main cavern and go forward from there.

"Getting stuck is part of writing into the dark," he writes. "Embrace the uncertainty of being stuck, trust your creative voice, give it a few moments' rest, and then come back and write the next sentence."

Stephen King is another author who tries to plot as little as possible. "I believe plotting and the spontaneity of real creation aren't compatible," he writes in *On Writing*. Instead, he sees himself as an archaeologist, uncovering stories like fossils buried in the ground. He starts his stories with a situation, with characters in a predicament, and then watches what happens and writes it down.

My very first published novel started with essentially that same exercise. I took a class from author Jeffrey Ford, who instructed us to all think of an interesting stranger we'd recently seen, then follow them in our imagination to see what they got up to. I remembered a woman I'd met on the bus the day before, Patricia, and started writing. I followed her as she got off the bus at the next stop and walked into a phở restaurant. I watched her sit down at a table with another woman—her sister, I realized—and perked up my ears as her sister asked Patricia for an unusual request: to help her resurrect her dead boyfriend. I kept following them, fascinated, until the resurrection went horribly awry and poor Patricia ended up possessed by the dead boyfriend.

I read that scene in class, and Jeffrey Ford told me, "If you don't write that novel, I'm stealing your idea."

I wrote the rest of the novel by the seat of my pants, following Patricia and her sister, Valeria, and the ghost of Dead Marco as they got deeper and deeper into trouble. And—somehow—I managed to uncover a pretty decent page-turner of a supernatural thriller. I painted myself into plenty of corners, but I came out unscathed on the other side.

Curtis Chen is another writer who likes to head into a story without much of the road map. "I like to think of it as improv," he told me. He generally has a setup for the story and some characters, and sometimes a vague idea of what he wants the ending to be. Then he asks himself what's the most interesting thing that could happen in a scene and starts writing.

"Part of the fun of that first draft is telling myself the story," he said. "I know I'm going to do a bunch of revising, so there's not so much at stake."

Earlier in his writing career, Curtis had tried outlining but found spending all the time on a detailed outline sucked away so much of his storytelling energy that he didn't have the drive to write the novel he'd outlined. With short stories, however, Curtis tends to do a lot more outlining. Having a plan of what he wants a specific story to do helps him zero in on what he wants to accomplish in every scene.

Over the years I've begun outlining more, but it's usually not until I've spent some time following the characters around to see what story they're telling me. If writing a single novel that way was nerve-wracking, writing a five-book series that way was downright terrifying. But having successfully landed them both, I'm a lot more trusting of my subconscious when it says, "Forget the roadmap, this is the direction to go. Trust me. We'll make it to the end."

Do I make wrong turns?

All the time.

And I know it when the writing is suddenly a lot harder. Dean Wesley Smith calls this being on the wrong path with the plot. When he gets bogged down, he knows his subconscious is trying to tell him he's going the wrong way, so he searches through what he's written until he finds the spot where he could have gone another direction, then he cuts off the extra words and strikes out fresh.

I debated whether I wanted to actually know this number, but I just checked the "cut scenes" file for the five-book Bulari Saga series, and it contains over 150,000 words. That's two complete novels worth of material that I wrote and didn't need because I was writing into the dark.

None of it was wasted writing, because it taught me the direction I didn't want to go. It showed me the dead ends. It made me more confident that I was going in the right direction. And, sometimes,

I was able to reuse scenes in later books or crib snippets of dialogue or descriptions.

I had fewer discarded words in later books as I got my bearings (and had even more practice feeling where a story should go). But if you write this way, you can't be afraid of writing extra words. It's all just part of your process.

Plotting

On the other end of the spectrum are the heavy outliners, who figure out every scene and beat of the story before they sit down to start drafting.

I was floored the first time I heard science fiction author Kevin J. Anderson say in a workshop that he writes detailed outlines that are sometimes over one hundred pages. Because he works so hard to develop his characters along with his plots, though, he rarely runs into the problem of having a character come to life and decide that his externally-imposed outline is rubbish. Having such detailed outlines is also critical for his writing process of dictating first drafts while hiking through the mountains of Colorado.

Fantasy author Brandon Sanderson, who writes sprawling epics, also leans more heavily to outlining in order to keep his books on course. As he writes in an article titled "Can You Go into Depth about Outlining?" on his website,[5] he follows what he calls a "points on the map" philosophy of writing, where he

---

5 "Can You Go into Depth about Outlining?" *BrandonSanderson.com*. October 14, 2018. faq. brandonsanderson.com/knowledge-base/can-you-go-into-depth-about-outlining/

creates increasingly detailed bullet points of parts, scenes, and beats that guide him through the writing process.

He starts by breaking his book into four parts and creating bullet points for each of the major plot points he already knows. Then, he looks at the major plot points and decides what needs to happen in order for them to occur, adding those scenes as bullet points in the outline. He also includes bullet points about character arcs and mystery/reveal arcs among the plot points so he remembers to seed those in as he writes.

"It means that my novels come out rather strong on the first draft, as I can foreshadow big events," he writes. "But, it also lets me innovate and change as I go, since the format of the outline is actually rather lax."

Fonda Lee also used a map analogy when she described her planning process to me. She starts with an outline and story structure to give her the confidence to start writing, knowing that it will likely change as she goes. "Then I throw it out, re-outline, throw it out, and re-outline again," she said. "It's having a map, but also knowing the map is only 50 percent complete."

With the third book of her Green Bone Saga, *Jade Legacy*, the story was so huge that she broke it into three parts and thought of it as seasons of a television show. She figured out the arc of Season One, wrote to the end of that part, then figured out Season Two, and so on.

Some writers will find it easier to stick to their outline throughout the entire course of the book, but if that's not you, that's alright. Like I mentioned, I need a certain amount of preplanning to know the direction I'm setting out in, but I really find the path when I'm in the middle of writing the book.

After years of being frustrated by this, a lightbulb went off for me when I met author Jordan L. Hawk at a conference. Jordan mentioned he only outlines the first half of the book because he always ends up throwing out the second half of the outline anyway.

Now, I do enough planning work to see the shape of the story—the beginning, the inciting incident, the midpoint, and the climax—and then write a more detailed outline for the first quarter of the book. Once I've drafted that first quarter and am happy with it, I outline the second quarter in greater detail, and so on.

Story Structure

Whether you feel most comfortable meticulously outlining or you prefer to tell yourself the story and see where it goes, you *do* need to have an understanding of story structure.

Rachael Herron, bestselling author, memoirist, and host of the *How Do You Write* podcast, told me how she learned about story structure. She'd gotten an MFA in creative writing without ever studying story structure and had accidentally managed to write a good organic structure with the first novel she sold—only to have her editor tell her that the second novel she turned in had no plot.

"I literally had to go away to a hostel on the coast, and I googled 'How to write a novel' and 'What is story structure?'," she told me. "I had to learn it the hard way."

Now, she counsels students to study and internalize story structure as early as possible, whether you plan your story ahead of time or impose structure on your draft later, as Rachael does.

So. What do we mean by story structure?

Basically, story structure is your story's beginning, middle, and end. The action starts, rises through a series of increasingly difficult challenges, reaches the climax, and resolves.

Different genres have different types of structures. Whether you're writing romance, fantasy, mystery, or literary novels, readers will be expecting you to include certain moments. Different cultures tend to have different story structures, as well. A Western structure such as the Hero's Journey might feel ubiquitous to a person raised on Star Wars movies and literary coming-of-age novels, but it's only one of many traditional story structures that can shape a writer's narrative.

Story structure is both universal and weirdly personal, and—as Rachael pointed out to me—different writing teachers will use different terminology to talk about the same concepts. Because of that, I'll keep this brief and point you in the direction of some solid resources below that you can use to find the way of thinking about story structure that resonates most with you, personally.

Ultimately, the best way to learn story structure is to thoughtfully consume, and write, as many stories as possible.

Understanding the Size of Your Idea

At this point, you may have an inkling of how big your idea is. Are you writing a book-length guide? A blog post? An article? A short story? A stand-alone novel? A ten-book epic fantasy?

Some writers are naturally drawn to a certain length of work. I have friends who primarily write short stories, while almost every short story I've tried to write reads like the first scene of a novel. My mind just automatically jumps to a big world with a massive conflict that demands to be spread out over 100,000 words.

There are two reasons to figure out the size of your idea ahead of time. You may be trying to figure out how big a box you need for whatever idea you already have. Or, you might have been given a box and told to put your idea inside of it. (For example, you've been asked to write a 900-word blog post, or you want to submit a short story to an anthology looking for stories of less than 5,000 words.)

If you have a brand new idea and no limitations on size, looking at the length and organizational structure of similar books, articles, or stories is one good way to understand how many words it might take to get your idea across.

If you're writing a nonfiction book, how many pages do similar books tend to have? How long are the chapters, and how many chapters are there? How many ideas is the author trying to get across in a book that length? How complex is the idea, and how much research have they done to support it?

If you're writing a short story or a novel, take a look at other stories in the markets you want to submit to. How long are they? How many characters are in the story? How many scenes and plot points? How big is the core conflict?

For example, if you're writing a thriller novel, you'll find that most of the ones in the market are going to have a single main storyline, and often one point of view. They tend to be shorter, maybe 65,000 to 80,000 words long. An epic fantasy novel, on the other hand, will probably have three or four (or more) point-of-view characters, each with their own storyline and major arc. It's not uncommon for epic fantasy novels to hit 150,000 words because of this.

Sometimes you don't know what you have until you get writing, and sometimes things change as you go. But familiarizing yourself with the sizes of containers similar ideas fit into will help you train your ability to figure out what you're writing.

It's also helpful because your audience will have certain expectations. No one wants to pick up a business book so full of fluff that should have been a couple of blog posts. Epic fantasy readers will be disappointed if your book is too short, and it'll be difficult to find an audience for your 250,000-word YA novel or memoir.

But what happens when you are given a box of a certain size and asked to fill it in? Then it becomes valuable to understand the factors that go into a piece of writing's length, so you can add and subtract.

Say you could talk for hours about growing your own food in the city, but you've been asked to write a short blog post. You need to cut your big idea down to the smallest piece of that conversation you can. In a blog post, you only have space to answer one small question like, "What are the best types of fruit trees for small backyards in Portland, Oregon?"

Conversely, if you had written that blog post and decided to write a book about it, start brainstorming everything that surrounds that idea. You talked about small backyards—what about large ones? What about plants other than fruit trees? Climates other than Portland?

For fiction, creating a story to fit the right box is all about adding or subtracting complexity. I tend to want to tell novel-sized stories, so even when I'm trying to write a short story, I tend to make them ridiculously complex. That's great if I am actually fishing for new novel ideas, because I can follow those threads and layer in sociopolitical turmoil and interpersonal conflict and character backstories to my heart's content.

But when I was writing a short story for one of Microcosm's Bikes in Space anthologies, I wanted to write a complete short story that landed at about 2,000 to 3,000 words.

I knew I wanted to write about a sphinx kitten and a girl mountain biker. The conflict would be about revolution, I thought. About the encroachment of mountain bikers on the sphinx population in the woods. There would be different factions among the sphinxes, and maybe the sphinx kitten and girl mountain biker would finally join forces to lead a revolution against—

I stopped myself. Factions? Revolution? That was a novel idea, not a short story idea.

I started over, trying to come up with the smallest conflict I could think of. My baby sphinx wanted to learn to fly and hadn't figured it out yet. She would learn with the help of the mountain biker.

That's an idea small enough to fit in a 2,000- to 3,000-word box.

PART TWO

DRAFTING

"A writer who waits for ideal conditions under which to work will die without putting a word on paper." —E.B. White

You've ideated. You've researched. You've come up with a plan.

Now it's time to write your first draft.

Of course, there's no one "right way" to write your first draft. The one constant is that you have to head into the word mines regularly and with intention, putting one word after the next, until your first draft is done.

It will be messy at first. It might take a while to see the shape of your story or argument. You'll take some wrong turns. You might do it all in one fast draft or revise as you go. The point is to do whatever you need to get through to that sweet, sweet pair of words: "The End."

In this section, we'll talk about where to begin your draft, how to get into the groove, what to do if you get stuck, and how to lock your inner critic out of your writing room.

But first, you might be wondering: have you done enough planning?

The distinction between "prep work" and "first draft" isn't always clear, and that's fine. What's important is to have enough planning done that you feel like you can start making confident progress, knowing that you may have to revisit the planning stage from time to time as you go through the draft.

With nonfiction, I need to have a decent amount of research and interviews done before I start to see the shape of the project, and finding its shape is important. (See the chapter on outlining nonfiction in the Planning section.) But I also take notes on my thoughts as I'm researching, and I may write a few paragraphs here and there—especially with a book like this, where I'm drawing a lot on my own personal experience. At times, I ended up drafting entire chapters because I got inspired by an interview or my research.

With fiction, drafting is a big part of how I discover things. I often don't know what the story is or who the characters are until I've let them run around a bit. Then, I'll often go back to the planning stage to map out a course and write until I need to go back to planning again.

Shonda Rhimes, the television producer and screenwriter behind *Grey's Anatomy* and *Scandal*, lets everything percolate in her mind before writing it all out in a rush when she has a complete idea. "There's a moment when I can't not talk about it anymore," she said in an interview with *Thrive Global*. "I can't not write about it anymore. . . . My brain is just excited to tell that story."[6]

6 "How Shonda Rhimes Starts Her Creative Process." *Thrive Global*. November 10, 2017. https://thriveglobal.com/stories/how-shonda-rhimes-starts-her-creative-process/

Barbara Kingsolver, on the other hand, ends up drafting tons of material that she knows she'll throw away. "It's just part of the process," she told the *Daily Beast*. "I have to write hundreds of pages before I get to page one."[7]

No one can tell you when you're ready to start drafting—it's something you'll feel in your bones.

7 "Barbara Kingsolver: How I Write." *The Daily Beast*. December 5, 2012. http://www.thedailybeast.com/articles/2012/12/05/barbara-kingsolver-how-i-write.html

WORKING THE WORD MINES

As with the other parts of the writing process, the best way to write your first draft is the one that gets you across the finish line with the least amount of frustration and (hopefully) the most amount of joy. There are no hard and fast rules except for one.

Go into the word mines and come back out with words.

Follow this one step as many times as you need to in order to come up with a completed draft.

You may write longhand in a library, you may type into a sophisticated word processing program or use a typewriter, you may dictate your first drafts each day during your commute like a friend of mine does. You may have thirty minutes at lunch every day, you may set aside one weekend day a week, you may be able to write full time.

Whatever working the word mines looks like to you, it's time to do it.

Some days you may strike a rich vein and feel like you could go for hours. Other days you may struggle to come up with a single sentence you like. There are no shortcuts, but there are best practices. Let's take a look at those.

Create the Brain Space

In *The War of Art: Break through the Blocks and Win Your Inner Creative Battles*, Steven Pressfield writes that he starts his day with the Invocation of the Muse from Homer's *Odyssey*. But it's not the prayer, or the lucky acorn from the battlefield at Thermopylae, or the lucky hooded sweatshirt he wears that make him have a productive writing day. It's the fact that he has carved out a sacred writing space. A series of cues that signal to his brain that this is writing time.

I don't resonate with the idea of evoking the divine—maybe because I write space mafia science fiction and B2B content marketing articles—but I resonate with the idea that your writing space should be sacred.

What do I mean by that?

If you want to be productive when you approach your work, you need to create a distraction-free environment that sets you up for success. Block the internet, shut your door, put in your noise cancelling headphones, let your family know you're in "do not disturb" mode, and write.

Maya Angelou famously kept a hotel room in her hometown that she paid for by the month, where she'd head every morning at 6:30 a.m. to write. Other writers may have an office or a quaint shed in the garden. But a dedicated writing space doesn't need to be a physical location. It can be as small and transient as any chair and table, and the place where your fingers connect with the keyboard.

After seven years freelancing, I finally have my own office and desk in a room where I can shut the door. But I travel enough to know I can't be reliant on that. I need to be able to create the optimal writing condition wherever I am.

A few years back, when coming off a frustratingly unproductive period of heavy travel, I met author Kevin J. Anderson at a conference. He'd just given a presentation talking about the twenty-plus conventions he'd attended that year and mentioned how many books he'd written while on the road.

I ended up standing next to him in line for lunch, and I asked him his secret to being actually productive while traveling so much.

"Three things," Kevin told me. "Bose noise-canceling headphones, so I can't hear the babies on the plane. Good sleep, so I can wake up early and write before I have to do anything else. And I will never again stay with a roommate when I go to a con. My writing time is worth more than the money I'd save."

As I was at that very moment frustrated with my con roommate situation, I understood his point.

I bought a set of Bose noise-canceling headphones that day and vowed never to sweat the extra cost of getting my own room when I was at a conference.

But more than giving me those three tips, the conversation got me thinking about my blockers and coming up with solutions rather than just wishing I was a more dedicated writer who could handle an adverse condition.

So, when the glare from the sun bothered me in the passenger seat on a road trip, I made Robert pull over at the next department store we saw so I could buy some of those baby sun shields for my window. When I realized I was so stressed about someone reading over my shoulder in public that I couldn't write on planes and in coffee shops, I bought a privacy filter for my laptop that I use when traveling.

And those noise-canceling headphones? Worth every penny. I pop them in my ears, turn on a thunderstorm from a free white noise app, and I'm immediately in work mode. While thunderstorms work for me, music might work for you. A lot of people recommend the app Focus@Will for focusing music, others curate playlists for every book and crank that up when they're looking for focus.

Curtis Chen is the one who introduced me to the idea of using an AlphaSmart Neo for distraction-free typing. The Neo is a portable, battery powered, word-processing keyboard originally made in the nineties to teach kids typing skills. It's basically a keyboard with a tiny screen that allows you to see four to six lines of text at a time.

The idea is that it's off the grid—so you can't get distracted by Twitter or whatever—and that the tiny screen makes rereading and editing a total pain. It forces you to stay focused and to keep going forward rather than puttering around with what you've already written.

(There are similar modern devices like the Freewrite, but you can pick up an old AlphaSmart Neo for thirty dollars.)

You can also use an app to keep you from digital distractions. I love Freedom, which you can set to block specific sites at certain times of the day. Forest is another fantastic app that allows you to set a timer and plant a virtual tree—if you look at your phone (or social media if you use the browser extension version), that virtual tree dies. Growing those little digital trees is incredibly motivating for me.

As I revise this book, it's fire season, and I keep turning off my Freedom app in order to check Twitter and see how friends who are evacuating across Washington and Oregon and California are doing. My phone is buzzing with texts and Slack messages from friends who are checking in with me. I'm writing a sentence, checking my email, writing a sentence, talking to my husband, writing a sentence . . .

The world is distracting, but mainly I am distracting myself because I've allowed phone notifications into my writing space. I've allowed myself to chase distracting thoughts. I've left my door open, which is the agreed-upon sign that my husband can come chat with me.

I've decided that—in spite of years of evidence—I can productively multitask today. But I can't. You can't. If writing is important to you, turn off your notifications, set a timer, and do nothing but this one task during your writing time.

When I'm writing on my Mac, I use Command+Tab to jump between windows. In the space between paragraphs, or when I get stuck on a sentence, sometimes my hand Command+Tabs automatically. When I do that on the Neo, nothing happens, and I'm forced to keep writing. (And when I'm working on my

Mac, I'll make sure that the window Command+Tab takes me to is something really boring, so I catch myself without getting distracted.)

I remind myself to go back in for one more paragraph, and I do.

Keep experimenting with what it takes to create a sacred space for your writing, and fight like hell to keep it. As Twyla Tharp writes in *The Creative Habit*, "The routine is as much a part of the creative process as the lightning bolt of inspiration, maybe more. And this routine is available to everyone."

When you establish a regular creative routine around your writing, it makes the time you spend with butt in chair (or recorder in hand) more productive. Your mind is limber and warmed up, and your subconscious takes the cue that now is the time to settle down and work.

Mine Those First-Draft Words

Every November, writers around the world participate in NaNoWriMo, or National Novel Writing Month. The goal is to write a complete-ish 50,000-word novel from start to finish over the course of that month. The prize is that you have written the first draft of your novel.

Curtis Chen is a fast drafter and taught himself to write this way by participating in NaNoWriMo for many years—and typing his first drafts on the AlphaSmart Neo. For Curtis, momentum on that first draft is key. If he decides to make a big change in the story, he just makes a note to add that into the first part of the story and continues writing forward.

Me? I always stall out during NaNoWriMo. Unlike Curtis, I can't easily lie to myself about the part that came before. I tend to write a draft of a scene one morning, spend the rest of the day mulling it over, then revise it the next morning before I start writing new material.

I also tend to get stuck at the end of every quarter of a novel. (Logistically, this is where you'll have a big turning point, so it makes sense.) I feel completely unable to move on until I've printed out what I've written so far, talked it over with Robert, re-outlined the book, and revised it. By the time I write the last quarter of the book, I have a solid idea of where I'm going and the drafting is usually much faster (and cleaner) than the earlier sections. After I write those magical words, The End, my first full pass of the novel is usually more of a polishing pass than a revising one.

Whether you write your first draft all in one go like Curtis or cycle through a few chapters at a time like me, your first draft words won't be pretty. And if you let your inner editor watch over your shoulder as you're puzzling that first draft out, you'll never get any forward momentum.

I tell myself that the second draft is when I get to build a beautiful sand castle, but first I have to fill the sandbox, and that means shoveling words in. I once heard Sean Platt, author and founder of Sterling & Stone, talk about drafting and revision at a conference where he told us, "Say it. Say it right. Say it well." The first draft is about getting the words out (say it). The second pass is about revising those words to make sure your story and message is coming across (say it right). The last pass is polishing up those words so they shine (say it well).

I have Sean's advice running on a constant loop when I'm in first-draft stage. "I just have to say it," I tell myself. Revision and polishing are for other passes altogether.

An early copywriting mentor of mine, Carol Tice, suggested approaching the first draft of an article like you're on a phone conversation with a friend. Say what's interesting about the story without consulting your notes because the parts that you remember are probably the most important parts to convey. You can flesh out the details later.

The reason this works is that stopping constantly to look things up slows you down. You may have a pile of research and great quotes, or you may be writing a novel and a recurring character comes in. Instead of stopping to check their eye color, or searching through your research for the exact right statistic, in your first draft, let yourself tell the story and leave a note to go back.

I will insert things in brackets with the letters TK which stands for "to come," a journalistic device, because there are no words in the English language that have those two letters next to each other, which makes it very easy to search for. For example, "Busting up a casino has never been at the top of Oriol Sina's bucket list, but here he is, standing in the middle of the [casino name TK] dressed for trouble in a suit he'd much rather be admiring on another man."

Because I do most of my writing in Scrivener, I will also use the comment feature to leave myself a note as to where I need to go back and fill in a detail. You might keep a notebook at hand and jot down things to research as they come up.

Whatever you do, you came here to write. There will be plenty of time for editing and research later.

Commit to Making Time

Real writers write every day.

Or do they?

For years, I told myself that if I wanted this author thing bad enough, I'd get those words written even on days that I'm sick, even on days that I'm too busy, even on days when I'm on vacation. I told myself that I was a complete slacker if I missed a day. That I wasn't a real writer if I didn't put in the time even when my brain and body were screaming for a break.

The result? A super unhealthy shame spiral around my writing process.

These days, I treat writing like the job that it is. I'm diligent about putting in the hours—but I also take vacations. I take breaks. I give myself the day off if I'm feeling sick, or if it would be more productive for my mental health to spend the day on something else instead.

Because that's how jobs work.

That mental shift has allowed me to be more productive on my writing days without losing momentum or burning myself out, and it really works for me.

Other people write every day and haven't missed a day in years. I'm always amazed by Sean Platt, who keeps up daily streaks for things like writing and reaching ten thousand steps that by now span years. It's impressive, and it works for him.

But streaks completely backfire for me. As soon as I miss a day I'm like, screw it, who cares. I'll meditate every day for twenty-seven days, accidentally miss a day, then not meditate again for a month because I broke my streak.

I got some insight as to why I do this when I read Gretchen Rubin's book *Better Than Before: Mastering the Habits of Our Everyday Lives.* (Which I highly recommend if you're trying to get into the habit of writing more regularly.) She develops a personality framework around habit formation called the Four Tendencies (which she later wrote a whole book about). One of the tendencies is Obligers, who tend to prioritize others' needs and expectations over their own (wow, this is me). For Obligers, creating external pressures can help them build good habits (like working with an accountability partner, or using a streak system). However, when Obligers start to get overwhelmed they can become resentful of these external pressures and throw them off in a fit of defiance. (And then feel shame for letting others down.)

That is me and streaks.

If I have the pressure of a streak looming over my head, I start to feel resentful. If I break it, I feel shame for letting down the streak. And I definitely don't need those negative emotions in my writing process.

In an essay for *Seven Scribes*, author Daniel José Older shares his take on whether or not you should write every day. He wrote his early novels while in grad school, working full time on an ambulance, teaching, and being present for his family.

"You can be damn sure I wasn't writing every day," he writes. "I got it all done because I found my flow, and I trusted it."[8]

One of the most intriguing parts of Older's essay is when he talks about what the mandate to write every day does to a writer's psyche. "Here's what stops more people from writing than anything else: shame. That creeping, nagging sense of 'should be,' 'should have been,' and 'if only I had . . .'" He goes on to say that shame, and the writer's block that follows, are the result of the message that real writers write every day.

A few friends and I have met together monthly for a few years as part of a mastermind group, which we call the Tiara Club. We all felt the Quarantine Angst of 2020 affecting our writing, and at one meeting we were exchanging strategies for getting back to work.

We'd all been struggling, but one friend in particular admitted he'd been forcing himself to sit down daily but was hating every one of the few words he managed to write. He seemed miserable, but he was determined to force his way through this mental block.

Another friend offered him a different idea. "What if you just tell yourself you're not a writer anymore?" he said. "What creative thing would you do if you didn't feel like you had to write? Do that thing. And maybe you'll end up writing, too, but if you don't, no big deal. Because you're not a writer this month."

8 "Writing Begins with Forgiveness: Why One of the Most Common Pieces of Writing Advice Is Wrong." *Seven Scribes*. September 9, 2015. sevenscribes.com/writing-begins-with-forgiveness-why-one-of-the-most-common-pieces-of-writing-advice-is-wrong/

He seemed reluctant, and at the end of that meeting his goals included writing every day.

Because that's what writers do. They write every day, no matter if they want to, no matter if it's fun, no matter if they feel inspired.

Right?

At the next month's meeting, though, this friend seemed happier. He said he'd actually tried the "tell yourself you're not a writer" suggestion. He'd let go of the "should-be-writings" and the shame of not meeting a daily quota—and it had been so freeing that he'd ended up writing more in his "nonwriter" month than he had in a while.

If writing every day motivates you, do it. But if it doesn't let it go and find some other way to get the work done. Maybe that's a weekly word count quota (which is what I do). Maybe it's looking at your calendar every Sunday and scheduling three hour-long sessions where they fit in your erratic life. Maybe it's the pressure of tracking a streak, so that you force yourself to get those words written before bed.

The best system of motivation to help you reach the end of this draft is the one that works for you, personally.

You don't have to write every day to call yourself a writer, just like you don't have to run every day to be a runner, or plumb every day to be a plumber. Though whether you're a write-every-day person or not, you'll see the best progress when you develop a regular writing routine and carve out the time.

Only you know if you're taking a well-needed break or procrastinating.

Only you know if you should be writing every day.

Pay attention to what you need, and get out of your own head about your process.

Where Should You Start Writing?

That seems like a question with a pretty straightforward answer: the beginning.

Only, it isn't always that cut and dried.

I've seen writers get so caught up in finding the perfect opening sentence or scene for their novel that they're paralyzed from going forward for weeks. Or writers who lose hours or days writing an introduction to their nonfiction book only to throw it out later.

That's why I say, begin where it's easiest.

Let's talk fiction for a minute. If you're earlier on in your writing career, chances are that you haven't developed a great sense of story structure yet, and what you think is the beginning actually isn't. That's fine—it just means you have the freedom not to get hung up on writing the perfect beginning. Just write!

Now that I have over a dozen finished books under my belt (some of which will never see the light of day), I've honed my sense of what makes a good opening scene. That means I'm pretty confident that where I start writing and where the book begins is the same place.

I like to write sequentially, so that I feel like I'm building on a solid base of story that came before. However, you may be one of those writers who jumps around.

Author and writing instructor Holly Lisle writes the ending scenes first so she knows where she's going and what elements she will need to have in place in order to get there. Then, she creates a handful of "candy-bar scenes"—the scenes you're just dying to write (the shoot-em-up escape, the marriage proposal, the supposed villain's change of heart). She makes sure those scenes are spread throughout the book, then writes down a single sentence for each—but doesn't allow herself to write them yet. They're called "candy-bar scenes" because you dangle them in front of you like a candy bar, knowing that once you write these next three scenes you'll get to write the one you've been excited about since the beginning of the book.

With nonfiction, I tend to bounce around. In writing this book, I drafted whatever chapter seemed most interesting in the moment and wrote sections as they came to mind (or were inspired by my research), moving the pieces around in my Scrivener project file as the draft started to take shape. When I'm working on an article, I'll do the same thing. Break it up into sections, then dive into whatever seems most interesting as the pieces begin to click into place.

When I'm writing nonfiction, there's no hard and fast rule except for one: never start with the introduction.

I may have an idea of what I want to say in the introduction, and I will often write a quick thesis to help guide what I'm writing next. But I find you don't always know what the book or article is about until you draft the rest of it.

If you're feeling stuck, start with whatever inspires you most. If that means you are writing a scene or a chapter or a subsection out of order, that's fine.

Simply begin wherever feels right to you.

Take Action

- Create space: Brainstorm your blockers. Finish the sentence: "I can't write because . . ." Now come up with a list of potential ways to get around that.

- Get rid of distractions: Create a plan to deal with distractions when you sit down to write. Put your phone in airplane mode. Turn off notifications on your computer. Shut your door or put on headphones. Set a timer. And write.

- Carve out time: look at your calendar and figure out when you can schedule writing sessions for the week.

- Head into the mines: No more excuses. Time to sit down and write—start in the middle if that's what works.

SILENCING YOUR CRITICAL VOICE

I didn't think much about critical brain versus creative brain until I spent a week on the Oregon Coast at a writing business masterclass with Dean Wesley Smith and Kristine Kathryn Rusch. Both were adamant about protecting the playful, creative part of your writing brain from the critical, analytical part—especially during the first draft.

I knew exactly what they were talking about, even if I didn't have language for it before then. For years, I'd had trouble letting myself "write poorly" because of my inner editor, but that had been drummed out of me when I started working as an in-house catalog copywriter and then as a freelance writer with tight deadlines. There was no time to let myself get blocked by my critical voice in my day job writing, and I'd become good at ignoring it in my fiction writing, too.

But when I raised my freelance rates enough that I could afford breathing room in between deadlines, I found myself with more time to write both fiction and nonfiction. And that critical voice started sneaking back in. I'd spend hours locked in worry that my first draft was too rough, that it wasn't hitting the right tones, that it was just plain bad.

It was all of those things, of course.

It was a first draft.

I'd just forgotten how to be okay with writing a fast and loose first draft out of necessity.

The way Smith writes about critical voice in *Writing into the Dark* really struck me: "Critical voice in humans is there to protect us. In writing, it wants to stop you from making a fool of yourself, or from putting out a bad product. . . . Made-up danger, of course, but to the writer letting the critical voice win, writing feels like very real danger."

In those times, I was letting my critical voice win. And you know what? It wasn't just slowing me down, it was making my initial draft worse.

Your thoughtful, critical brain is valuable when you're planning and researching. It's useful when you're thinking about your audience and what form you want your piece to take. It's going to be a great help in the revision and editing stage.

But you know when your critical brain isn't helpful?

Right now, when you're drafting.

Right now, when you need to trust your gut and get out of your own way.

Right now, when you're trying to tap into your subconscious to understand what story you want to tell.

When you get your critical voice out of the way and let your creative brain tell the story, you may not end up with the finest prose on the first take—but you'll end up with something better. You'll end up with real nuggets of gold that your critical brain can work into a masterpiece.

In *Writing into the Dark*, Smith points out that things like theme, subtext, and all that good English major stuff we're taught should be part of Good Literature doesn't come about because authors sit down and map it out. "Let me be clear here," Smith writes, "My critical brain is not smart enough to put all that stuff in. Luckily for me, my creative brain seems to be smart enough if I get my critical brain out of the way and let it."

The biggest moments of chill when I'm revising come when I've trusted my subconscious—not when I've planned something out. My planned twists and reveals always feel flat. But those moments that slip out during the drafting process when I let myself go, those are magic.

After I turned in Bulari Saga 5, I sat down and reread the first four books in order to catch any inconsistencies, and because I hadn't really had a chance to experience it all as a full story. And along the way I kept coming upon tiny seeds I'd planted in earlier books that I'd completely forgotten about, which gave me chills when I realized how my subconscious had paid them off at the climax of the story.

So now that I've hopefully convinced you to turn off your critical voice, how do you do it?

When I first started writing this section, I thought of maybe three ways to do it. I dusted my hands off, feeling smug.

Then, on a whim, I tossed this question out to Twitter: "How do you silence your critical voice when you're writing?"

Wooo, boy, did people have Thoughts!

I invite you to try one or all of the following tricks to get your critical voice to shut it.

Remember That No One Writes Amazing First Drafts

Adonia Lugo told me how she has a tough time with first drafts and often struggles with the impulse to polish first-draft sentences. She learned an unforgettable lesson in college when a professor showed her a first draft of one of her own articles. "It was terrible," she said. Words were misspelled, sentences were in fragments, but she could understand the argument. "It was a confidence booster to see that her early draft wasn't professional work."

Joanna Penn said that when she began writing fiction, she didn't realize how big a part the editing process would play and would get stuck on how bad her sentences were compared to her heroes'.

"Most writers won't see anyone else's first draft," she told me. "You think, oh my goodness, Margaret Atwood's my favorite writer, and my first draft doesn't look anything like that! But no one is born a great writer. It's about practice and persistence. It's about learning your craft and editing that book."

Sometimes you just need a reminder that your first draft isn't supposed to be brilliant. Author Jordan L. Hawk threw out two tricks on Twitter that help him remember that bad is the point of the first draft. First, he puts a sticky note that says "discovery draft" on the side of the monitor. Second, whenever a sentence seems particularly awful he writes [ugh] and keeps going. "Spoiler alert," Jordan wrote, "I almost never edit those because they're never actually that bad."

Remember. When you're drafting, getting ideas out—not brilliance—is the goal.

Visualize—and Neutralize—Your Critical Voice

In *Bird by Bird*, Anne Lamott talks about quieting the critical voices in her head as being half the battle of sitting down to write. She uses this visualization exercise:

Close your eyes and wait for the chatter to start up, then isolate the voices individually (your parents, friends, past writing teachers, other critics) and visualize the person speaking as a mouse. "Pick it up by the tail and drop it into a mason jar," she writes. Keep doing this until all the mice are in the mason jar—then put the lid on.

Finally, Lamott writes, imagine the jar has a volume knob. "Turn it all the way up for a minute, and listen to the stream of angry, neglected, guilt-mongering voices. Then turn it all the way down and watch the frantic mice lunge at the glass, trying to get to you. Leave it down, and get back to your shitty first draft."

Dean Wesley Smith visualizes his critical voices as "a tiny little thing whimpering off in a corner of my mind. When it tries to stand up, I throw bricks at it until it goes back to its corner and leaves me the hell alone."

I have a similar image of my critical voice, though instead of throwing bricks, I envision it as an annoying toddler needing to be distracted so I can get the work done. I joked once that you just need to give your inner critic a lollipop and tell it to sit in the corner, and I loved the visual so much I asked my friend, artist Nalisha Rangel, to draw it for me. It hangs by my desk.

In a similar exercise, essayist Salman Ansari commented on Twitter that he will sometimes write a quick set of bullets above the outline of an essay to note any concerns he has: "I usually label it 'Parrot Says What?' We want to acknowledge them without taking them too seriously."

Salman went on to note that putting concerns on the list doesn't make them silly or inconsequential—for example, your critical voice may be expressing a valid criticism you could receive. When you write down the worry rather than ignoring it, your mind stops obsessing on it, and you can do the work. Later, when it's time to think about those concerns, you'll be prepared.

Get a Change of Scenery

Moving locations can physically put your mind in one state or another. If I'm having trouble turning off my critical brain, I'll sometimes go write on the couch or go to a coffee shop. It gets me away from the desk where my to-do list lives and helps me break out of that critical mindset.

I know other writers who are regimented about it, doing all of their first draft writing in one location (the kitchen table, an armchair, a desk) and doing all of their editing, emails, and business-minded work from another physical location.

The location doesn't have to be physical. A friend of mine even created two logins for her laptop, one that has access to all the programs she uses in her regular life, and another login that's restricted to just her word processing program. When she logs in to the latter, her critical brain gets the message that it's time to write.

Practice Low-Stakes Writing

If your critical voice is getting hung up on the fact that you're working on your magnum opus, and it must be incredible, try warming up with something that doesn't feel so important. Set a timer and write nonsense for twenty minutes, or begin each day with the morning pages exercise from Julie Cameron's *The Artist's Way: A Spiritual Path to Higher Creativity*, writing three pages longhand, stream of consciousness.

I find that my critical voice can be triggered even by the tools I use. I have a whole stack of nice journals that I've been gifted over the years, but I can't write in any of them without feeling like it has to be Important and Wise. Instead, I prefer to jot down random notes and thoughts and bad first draft prose in those spiral-bound notebooks you can buy for fifty cents each. When I open up one of those, I feel free to write in a way that I don't with a nice journal.

Just Get Going

Most of the people who responded to my question about critical voice on Twitter had the same point: The best way to get your critical voice to go away is to just get started and lose yourself in the project. Bribe yourself with a treat, maybe a cup of coffee or tea, a piece of chocolate, maybe a special snack that you only get during writing sessions.

Or, bribe yourself by allowing yourself to work on whatever part of your manuscript seems the most fun at the moment. Are you dying to write a scene a few chapters ahead? Let yourself tell that story. Are you hung up on one part of your thesis but can't stop thinking about another? Write the fun bits, and let that momentum silence the critical voice for you.

I find that setting myself a timer for twenty-five minutes and telling myself that I only have to work for that long is often enough to get me past that initial stumbling block of getting started. Once that timer goes off, I'm often in the groove enough that I ignore it and keep writing.

In the end, quieting your critical voice will get easier as you practice. But it won't go away.

As Steven Pressfield writes in *Turning Pro: Tap Your Inner Power and Create Your Life's Work*, "Each day, the professional understands, he will wake up facing the same demons, the same Resistance, the same self-sabotage, the same tendencies to shadow activities and amateurism that he has always faced. The difference is that now he will not yield to those temptations. He will have mastered them, and he will continue to master them."

Keeping Your Critical Voice from Silencing You

Your critical voice doesn't only show up when you're forming imperfect sentences. It can also try to dull the edges of the story you're trying to tell.

After all, it's trying to keep you safe. And writing the truth doesn't feel very safe.

I didn't see how this affected me until very recently. I thought I just wrote stories about ghosts, and tree-dwelling fantasy people, and space mafiosos. They have adventures, and they also grapple with big, universal questions: How do societies heal after centuries of injustice? How do friendships heal after deep betrayals? What are we willing to do for our faith? How many sacrifices for our individual freedom are too many?

But I didn't think I was writing about *myself*.

That very scary task was left to friends who studied creative nonfiction and wrote memoir and essays and poetry. I wrote about spaceships and gun battles. I was safe.

It wasn't until about halfway through the Bulari Saga that I began to do some thoughtful self-work and started to recognize certain patterns and constructs and fears I personally have. And, in horror, I saw how I was working those out on the pages of the Bulari Saga. In public. In front of my mom, my dad, my friends, the whole damned world.

It was mortifying and fascinating.

Later, when a friend asked me what that third book of the Bulari Saga was about, I joked, "It's about a bunch of people struggling with self-worth issues who are completely overworked and anxious. Everyone says to write what you know!"

(The book also has tense political intrigue, gun battles and car chases, a hardboiled detective, a marriage proposal that still makes me giddy, and a delightfully vicious villain. But it was clearly written at a time when I was very stressed out.)

When your critical voice is dulling the edges of your writing, that voice often shows up in the form of another person. You worry about what your parent will think when they read your memoir. If your spouse will think this line in your poem is about them. If your former boss will recognize an anecdote, if your sibling will stumble across your blog and out you to the rest of your family before you're ready.

When those voices are in your head as you write this first draft, you'll find yourself holding back from what you really want to say.

Your gut instinct may be to make one choice with a character, but a voice in your head is screaming, "Nononono, if you do that people will instantly think *X* about you!" Your critical voice wants to protect you. But writing your truth is a gift you give to the world. Listening to that critical voice means the person who may need that gift the most may never get it.

Using a pen name is a great way to say what you need to say. I know people who write under pen names for tons of reasons—they don't want their grandparents to find their blog about losing their religion, they don't want their students' parents to know they write erotica, they're not ready to come out to the world as trans but they're exploring it in fiction, they just want to write violent, pulpy space pirate adventures without catching flak from their poetry major friends.

I mentioned at a workshop that I was struggling a bit with getting other people out of my head as I wrote. What would my [mom/grandma/sister/cousin] think of all the [swearing/gay characters/violence/whatever]? It was suggested I publish them under a pen name, because then I could write my truth without the worry that people I know would read it.

I hadn't yet realized how much of myself I was putting in these books, but I did know one thing: I bounced *hard* off the idea of writing under a pen name.

If I was going to write things that felt true to me, I didn't want it to be because I hid it from those closest to me. I wanted to learn how to be vulnerable and honest, knowing that they would read it. In fact, *because* they would read it.

(This isn't to say you shouldn't write under a pen name—there are lots of really good reasons to use one. But it felt wrong for me.)

Whether or not you choose to publish under a pen name is a different decision—but for now, tell yourself that you have that option during the first draft stage if it helps you dig deeper into your own truth.

Todd Henry writes in *Die Empty*, "We don't grow by simply doing what's expected of us. If we stay squarely in our comfort zone, where we are perfectly capable and confident, we may never discover and develop our hidden aptitudes."

But it's not just about developing your own skill as a writer. When you make the hard choices, the true choices, you create something that transcends simple words.

Later on in the Bulari Saga series, when I'd finally owned up to the fact that I was dealing very publicly with my own issues by forcing my characters to go through them, I came up against a choice I nearly shied away from.

A character my protagonist loved deeply was going to die.

When I'd first planned the scene, it seemed like a good choice. But by the time I got to writing it, I'd spent a season watching family members age and trying to figure out how to deal with the grief of their eventual passing. My grandfather was in hospice. My grandma had just had a stroke, and we weren't sure if she would recover. I was starting to realize that my own parents had health issues.

I didn't want to write such a tragic scene. I didn't want my mom to have to read it while I knew she was also grieving. I talked about it with my sister and almost decided that it wasn't the time to write it because my own personal grief was still too close to the surface.

But, I also knew that made this the perfect time to write about loss.

I wrote the scene, unable to see the words on the screen because I was crying the entire time. In editing, I knew I'd made the right decision. Shortly after I published that book, I heard from a friend who'd recently lost a family member. He told me it was the first "death scene" he had come across since. He wrote: "You did a wonderful job there, and it opened up some good grief for me. I'm needing to find ways to access it, so thank you, sincerely, for gifting me with that."

If I had shied away from making that terrifying choice, I would've never given him that gift. Hopefully it's a gift for others who are processing grief, as well.

Don't let your critical voice silence your gifts.

Take Action

Are your fingers hesitating over the keyboard because of some secret inner voice telling you you're not good enough or that the world will point their fingers at you for what you're about to write?

Try one of the suggestions discussed above to silence that voice:

- Write "Bad First Draft" at the top of the page or on a sticky note on your computer.

- Do a visualization exercise to help banish that voice and neutralize its power.

- Change locations so you're not sitting where you normally work on "serious" things.

- Start with a low-stakes exercise, like typing a page of rubbish or journaling before digging in to your draft.

- Set a timer for twenty-five minutes and tell your critical voice it can come back once the timer dings.

- Go complain on Twitter that you're feeling stymied by imposter syndrome (kidding about this one, but use #WritingCommunity and you'll quickly get a reminder that you're not alone!).

GETTING UNSTUCK

There's a moment in every book when I don't know if it will ever be finished. A moment where I'm exhausted, overwhelmed by the enormity of the project, and hopelessly lost in the plot.

These moments are normal, and fine. And every time it happens, I remember that I've been here before, I've done this before, and I've gotten through it.

And you can, too.

I first heard about the different types of energy you feel at different stages of a project from Joanna Penn. She talks about the starting energy, the excited honeymoon period of knowing you have an idea and getting into it. There's the finishing energy when you're wrapping up a project and getting it out the door. But in between, you need the pushing-through energy to actually ship it.

"I think one of the biggest problems writers who don't finish books have is thinking that their starting energy will carry them through all the way to the end," Joanna told me. The excitement that got you going will eventually fade.

Here are some ideas to help get yourself through that push.

Figure Out Why You're Stuck

First up, figure out what's got you stuck. Are life circumstances getting in the way? Have you lost your motivation? Did you take a wrong turn while you've been writing into the dark, and your subconscious is trying to tell you that?

I have a journal file in the Research section of every Scrivener project, and that's where I turn when I get stuck. I open that file and jot down how I'm feeling about the project, where I'm feeling stuck, any fears or hopes. Sometimes I include a bit about my day or overall mental state. Normally it helps me figure out where I got off track.

If I'm feeling stuck in the middle of a writing session, I'll open that document and just ramble on until I write my way out of my funk, and the creative juices get flowing again. Just telling myself the story without worrying what it sounds like helps things make sense again. I just scrolled back through my journal document for the five books of my Bulari Saga series, and there are some entries that stop mid-sentence because whatever problem I had suddenly solved itself.

A lot of writers do this longhand in a physical notebook, which is a wonderful way to go. It takes you away from the computer and puts you into a completely different mental space.

Leave Yourself a Crumb Trail

Ernest Hemingway famously stopped his writing sessions mid-sentence so that when he sat down at the typewriter the next day he already had his next prompt ready to go. I worry I'd forget what I was going to say, but I definitely agree that it's easier to get back in the groove at the beginning of a session when you've left yourself notes from the session before.

In *Start Finishing*, Charlie Gilkey calls this a crumb trail. He recommends taking a few minutes at the end of your block of work to leave yourself a few notes about where you should get started next time. Don't just assume that you will remember the brilliant thought you had, or that you will remember the direction that you were going in. Plan to get lost, and expect that life might get in the way.

"The irony is," he writes, "that once you assume you'll be lost at the start of the next focus block and prepare for it by leaving bread crumbs, it becomes significantly harder to be lost at the start of your next focus block. Once leaving bread crumbs becomes a habit, daily momentum becomes a reality."

Refill the Creative Well

At the beginning of the COVID-19 pandemic, it was hard to feel creatively inspired about anything. After fighting with an increasingly frustrating inability to write, I finally tapped out and spent three days binge reading a series of serial killer thrillers (the *Stillhouse Lake* series by Rachel Caine). It was nothing like what I was writing, and it was so absorbing that I completely stopped worrying about the fact that I didn't feel creative.

At the end of those three days, I closed the last book, peeled myself out of the armchair, went for a walk, and realized that I knew how the last book of the Bulari Saga was going to end.

Pounding my head against my computer for three weeks hadn't helped me write again. Three days of binge reading did.

In *Die Empty*, Todd Henry writes about the state of "creative inversion," when more creativity and ideas are flowing out of you than in. The creative process is all about combining ideas around us into something unique. "When we are inverted," he writes, "we have fewer options to smash together because we've either (a) not been spending enough time seeking inspiration or (b) we need to spend more time processing our experiences to mine them for potentially useful insights."

Your brain needs creative input and inspiration, and it needs the time to process these things and synthesize something new. If you've been running along at breakneck speed without taking the time to refill your creative well, that might be the reason you're stuck.

When I'm stuck on a plot point, Robert often suggests action movies we could watch for inspiration.

Todd Henry recommends that you don't just search aimlessly for inspiration, but keep questions in mind about what you hope to learn from what you're consuming.

Reconnect with Your Why

Do you remember why you started working on this project in the first place?

Because you want to tell a fun story. Because you want to share the lessons you've learned. Because you wish you'd had this guide when you were younger. Because you want to make a difference. Because you want to prove to yourself you can do it. Because you want to share these characters with the world.

When you're stuck, it's a great time to go back to your *why*. Reminding yourself what got you so excited about the project in the first place is the best way to keep your focus during the inevitable slog in the middle.

Spend some time interrogating why you want to work on this particular project—and don't worry if it's not grandiose and altruistic!

For example, my motivation for writing this book is partly to help inspire other writers and partly because I'm getting a kick out of the speaking I've started to do as a result of *From Chaos to Creativity*, and I want to have a strong follow-up book that can keep opening doors.

On the other hand, my motivation for writing my next series, the Nanshe Chronicles, is purely that "space pirates meets *Indiana Jones* meets *Leverage*" sounds like a whole hell of a lot of fun to write.

Understanding—and staying connected to—the why is an important part of the writing process for Fonda Lee. "You have to live with it for so long, especially as a traditionally published author of very long books," she told me. "It's really important with every project to keep the love of that project front and center because that's what pushes you through the not so fun parts of the process."

Rachael Herron put it this way: "I'm growing a flower garden for the first time in my life and bringing the flowers into the house. These flowers would not exist had I not put the seeds in the ground, and this book would not exist had I not sat down and made some stuff up. Participating in that almost elemental magic of writing really gets me through the hard days."

Think about what you'll get out of finishing. Is it the personal pride and satisfaction? If you're writing professionally, it might be the money or the deadline.

And it's not just about you. Whether you're writing fiction or nonfiction, there's some reader out there who's waiting to read your work, Charlie Gilkey told me. "Hopefully I know who that reader is. I know that if I flail around another six weeks, that's six weeks more that person may not be able to get this thing they need. Because fundamentally, it's not so much about me. It's about what this work does for the world."

Remember your ideal reader—either the real-life one, or the one you imagined. They're waiting to read your words. They *need* to read them.

So sit back down and write.

Take Action

If you're feeling blocked try one of these techniques to get yourself back in the writing mindset once more:

- Open up your journal and freewrite about your mindset: What is keeping me from this project? What made me so excited about this project in the first place? What are my dreams for it? What are my fears?

- Alternatively, try freewriting about the project itself: What's missing from the draft so far? What's the most interesting thing that could happen next? What will readers take away from this book? Is there an earlier part of your draft you need to shore up so that you can move forward?

- Keep your momentum by leaving yourself breadcrumbs between sessions. Write a few sentences about where you're heading next, or leave yourself a voice memo at the end of every writing session.

- Refill the creative well by losing yourself in a fun book, heading to a gallery or museum, listening to a podcast, watching inspiring movies, or listening to lectures or courses related to your topic.

- Reconnect with your *why* by asking yourself these questions: What was the initial spark of this project? Who most needs to read this once it's done?

FINISHING THE DRAFT

I have a friend, Israeli freelance writer Ayelet Weisz, who has slowly but surely trained me to celebrate. For years, we were in a small accountability group together, and any time one of us would post a big milestone, her response was invariably, "Congratulations! What are you doing to celebrate?"

"It's just a small thing. There's so much work left to do," was my usual response.

But to Ayelet, it didn't matter that the work was far from over. What mattered was getting me to promise her that I would celebrate the milestone.

You *have* to celebrate. But it can be tough to know exactly when to celebrate. Do you celebrate completing the first draft? Turning it in to your editor? Publication?

Yes, yes, and yes.

The writing process can be a slog, so the first thing Ayelet and I think you should do once you've finished a draft is to do something special for yourself. Tell the world about it! Tell your friends! Tell your pet! Pop open that nice bottle of wine or buy yourself that pastry you've had an eye on. It doesn't have to be big, but it should feel special.

Then put your manuscript away for a bit and give yourself space for reflection.

Now that you're done with your first draft, you may be tempted to rush right into the revisions and editing. Or you may never want to see it again—I get it. Either way, you need to give yourself some time away from the draft before you dive right back in.

Rest and reflection is useful even on a small project. When I am writing an article, I generally intend to have the final draft done the day before it's due. That way I can spend time on it the next day with fresh eyes to see if the argument makes sense and clean it up. If I am on an abbreviated schedule—or haven't left myself enough time—I will at least leave a lunch break, or go for a long walk in between the first full draft and the final draft that I turn into my client. You need that mental space.

Giving yourself space helps you reset your view of your first draft, so you can go in with fresh eyes. It'll help you see problems—and strengths—more clearly.

What should you do while you're making space? If you've been on a big push to finish, now's a good time to take stock of your life. Are there things that you've been letting lapse? People you want to talk to? Other outlets or hobbies that you've been putting aside? A massive to-do list of things you've been ignoring?

Take a big, deep breath of recovery, and pat yourself on the back before you turn the page and start in on the next phase of the project: revisions.

Take Action

Set aside time to reflect on the drafting process. What went well, what setbacks, challenges, or missteps did you experience, what did you learn, what habits, practices, or routines do you want to keep going forward?

Oh—and don't forget the most important step. Do something to celebrate finishing your draft!

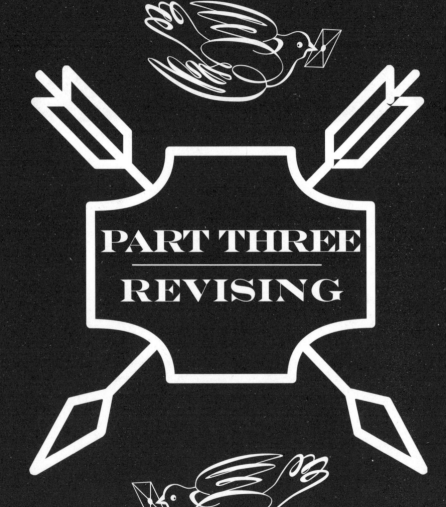

PART THREE

REVISING

"Storytellers and poets spend their lives learning that skill and art of using words well. And their words make the souls of their readers stronger, brighter, deeper."
—*Ursula K. Le Guin*

All righty. You've written The End on your first draft. You treated yourself in celebration, and you've taken some time to rest and reflect.

It's time to whip this mess into a finished product.

I first heard Rachael Herron talk about revision at a conference, and I was struck by how much enthusiasm she had for a subject most writers dread. As someone who also loves revisions, I knew I had to ask her why this part of the writing process was her jam.

"I love revision because I'm such a control freak," she told me. "The first draft feels like you're cartwheeling clumsily down a snowy hill, and I don't like being out of control. But revision is where you find out what your book really wanted to be in the first place. It feels more creative to me."

The revision process can feel overwhelming and messy and impossible, whether you're approaching it for the first time or the twentieth. But it's in revisions that you move your draft slowly but surely from an unruly mess to something resembling the Platonic ideal of a book you've been holding in your mind.

Fonda Lee put it in a way that I can't stop thinking about. "I always have this bright, shiny idea of how great the story is going to be," she told me. "And to me, first drafting is just moving further and further away from that vision because everything you write sucks. But then once there's something to fix, it feels more like things are going up. I love the whole process of improving and sanding and polishing."

I feel the same way. I even love the line editing pass that many other writers hate, because that's when I feel like I'm doing the story justice. In nonfiction, that's where I know I'm making a strong argument, and my point is razor sharp.

That's when I get chills.

Khaled Hosseini, author of *The Kite Runner*, is also in our club, and he says it more profoundly than I can, "A first draft is really just a sketch on which I add layer and dimension and shade and nuance and color. Writing for me is largely about rewriting. It is during this process that I discover hidden meanings, connections, and possibilities that I missed the first time around. In rewriting, I hope to see the story getting closer to what my original hopes for it were."[9]

9 "Khaled Hosseini: How I Write." *The Daily Beast*. November 7, 2012. .thedailybeast.com/articles/2012/11/07/khaled-hosseini-how-i-write.html

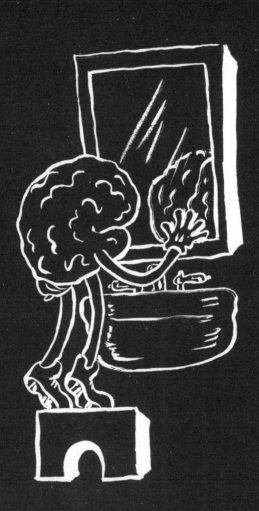

FOUR STEPS TO REVISION

Many writers get stuck in the enormity of revision—it can give you whiplash to go from the joy of finishing your first draft to the sinking realization that you still have so much work ahead of you. But as Rachael Herron likes to point out, revision is a learnable process with a toolbox of techniques you can use every single time. Once you have those tools in hand, revising your draft will seem much less overwhelming.[10]

In this section, we'll be talking about revising and editing as two separate steps, starting from the big picture view and slowly zooming in to tackle smaller and smaller problems.

Think of it as a vaguely four-step process:

1) Rediscover and develop the core idea in your draft.

2) Fix the major problems in your draft so the core idea shines through.

3) Revise at a scene/section level to support the core idea.

4) Edit at the sentence level to make your draft gleam.

---

10 For a great overview of Rachael's revision process, check out her book, *Fast-Draft Your Memoir: Write Your Life Story in 45 Hours.*

Whether you're writing fiction or nonfiction, you'll be following the same basic principles. While you may catch some grammar and spelling errors in the revision stage, don't worry much about them. Focus instead on the big-picture structure questions before you get nitpicky about word choice.

You want to go through a revision and editing pass before you hand it off to outsiders. If you have an alpha reader (see the section on early readers) you might let them see it at this stage. But generally you don't want to inflict your first draft on anyone but yourself.

Depending on your drafting process, the amount of revision you may need at the end can vary. Joanna Penn is so solid on her story that she doesn't end up doing much in the way of revisions. Especially as she writes longer series, where she knows the thriller structure and her characters well enough to write clean drafts.

In my case, I've already mentioned that I cycle back through my draft and revise it at roughly every quarter mark before drafting the next quarter. By the time I have a complete draft, it doesn't require many structural changes, which means that I only need to make minor revisions to the final quarter before I do a self-editing pass and ship it to my editor.

That's the method I ended up with by the end of the Bulari Saga series. But I wrote the first book in the series, *Double Edged*, three full times from scratch. The first time, I realized I was writing two stories in one—a social-justice story about a teacher on a strange planet plus a shoot-outs-and-intrigue mafia story. The second time, I tried to cut out the mafia story to focus on the teacher, but spun my wheels until I realized I really just wanted to write a space mafia book.

At the end of that third draft, I thought I'd nailed it—only to give it to Robert and have him tear it apart in terms of character motivation, pacing, and structure. After a massive revision pass that felt like I'd torn it all apart *again* and was stitching it back together, I finally came up with a book that worked.

All that to say that revision—like everything in the writing process—will be different for every person. And likely different for every project. As with everything, err on the side of doing what feels the best to you and gives you the most joy.

(And, yes, revision can give you joy!)

Let's get started.

Rediscovering the Core Idea

Chances are your first draft seems pretty disjointed. Maybe you knew what you wanted to say when you started, or maybe you figured it out as you wrote. Or maybe you thought you were saying one thing and ended up saying something else.

Whatever the case, the time to take stock of your core idea, or theme, is *now*. It's the theme you defined early on in planning, but it may have changed along the way. This rediscovery and refining will become the organizing principle around which you'll end up revising your work.

For instance, you may discover nuance in that main theme that will help you create something even more unique. With this book, the theme went from "How do you write a book?" to "How do you create a writing process that brings you joy?"

With nonfiction, your theme is probably pretty obvious—it's the question you're trying to answer for your readers. How can I live a more sustainable lifestyle by growing my own food? How can I finish more projects? What should I do when I visit Lima, Peru?

What might be less obvious in nonfiction is your *story*. How are you leading your reader through your book in a way that best answers that question?

When Adonia Lugo was first working on her PhD dissertation, she'd been doing fieldwork for two years and felt like the material needed to be presented in the chronological order in which it took place. Her dissertation advisor told her that it wasn't dishonest to move the material around, as Adonia had thought. Instead, sometimes that was the best way to create compelling arguments and conclusions.

Later, when she was turning her dissertation into *Bicycle/Race*, her editors encouraged her to think of herself as a character with an arc. The result is a book about race, urban infrastructure, and bicycling advocacy with a compelling coming-of-age arc based around Adonia's own experience.

"Sometimes what's 'true' comes through differently in story than in writing just a list of facts," Adonia told me. "I'm still learning how to actually put that into practice."

With fiction, I like to think of theme as the question you're asking, rather than the moral or point you're trying to make. Your story may wrestle with multiple questions. Try to choose the one that calls to you the most, and don't worry about trying to make it sound profound. Any famous story can be distilled down to something pretty trite: obsession will ruin your life, empathy will overcome fear, justice will prevail.

Make your theme as simple as possible. In *The Secrets of Story: Innovative Tools for Perfecting Your Fiction and Captivating Readers*, Matt Bird writes, "Remember, the goal of a rewrite should always be to simplify the story, not complicate it. The ultimate goal should be to have a simple story about complex characters, and not vice versa."

Even a novel as sprawling as Stephen King's *The Stand* has a very simple thread at the heart of it. In *On Writing*, King tells a great story about getting completely stuck halfway through the draft. He mulled over his tangled plot lines for weeks before hitting on exactly what he was trying to say with the book as a whole, "All this suggested to me that violence as a solution is woven through human nature like a damning red thread." He wrote the second half of the draft in a fury, then revised the second draft with that theme in mind.

"I was astounded at how really useful 'thematic thinking' turned out to be," he writes, going on to add, "Since my revelation . . . I have never hesitated to ask myself, either before starting the second draft of a book or while stuck for an idea in the first draft, just what it is I'm writing about."

Having trouble figuring out the theme of your novel? Rachael Herron pointed out that the theme of your story is probably the same as your favorite books and movies. (Her theme tends to be mother-daughter relationships and/or the idea that family is chosen.)

When Rachael begins her revision, she writes her theme on a sticky note and sticks it on her computer. It's a visual reminder as she's revising that every scene should reflect, as she put it, at least a small ray from the beam of light that is her theme.

For example, if she's writing a book about a mother-daughter relationship and her characters are having an argument in the shopping mall, she'll take a look at what's in the background of the scene. She may have written six teenagers roughhousing in the first draft; in the revision she might change the teens to a kid racing away from her mother's hand as the mother reaches out to catch her.

"The theme should never be heavy-handed," she told me. "The reader shouldn't notice that it's happening, and it should even be hard for you to see as a writer. It's more of a grace note, or an aroma that's in the air."

Fixing the Major Problems

Now that you have your core idea/theme/point nailed down, it's time to remake your first draft with that end goal in mind.

Rachael Herron calls the second draft the "make sense draft," in that it just has to make a little more sense than the first draft did. Right now, don't worry about spelling and grammar errors, don't worry about your descriptions and metaphors and prose. In this draft, you're taking the raw material of your first draft and shaping it into something that resembles the shining, perfect book in your mind.

You've got this.

Reading through your first draft might surprise and delight you. It might make you cringe. Your prose may be better than you remember, or it may totally suck—and either way is fine. Your draft is about to go through a transformation into something incredible, and the revision process is the chrysalis that makes it all possible.

At this stage, Rachael made the excellent suggestion to save an entirely new file. When I know a scene or section is in for a big revision, I'll often copy the files into an "OLD VERSION" folder in Scrivener, or use the snapshot feature to save a historic record of the original version.

(I have only once or twice ever gone back to look at those old files, but it sure does feel good to know they're there!)

Read through Your Draft and Catalog Problems

Before you can begin to fix anything in your draft, you need to take stock of what you have and what your major problems are. And that means reading back through your draft—especially if you haven't looked at certain chapters for a while.

Print out the whole thing and sit down with a nice beverage, a stack of colored pens, and sticky notes. Printing out your draft is best because it lets you read through without succumbing to the temptation of fixing things as you go. (If you can't ignore typos, suggested Rachael, put a checkmark next to the line that needs to be fixed and move on.)

Printing it out can also help you create mental distance between yourself and your work, Fonda Lee noted. "I try to think of my own work as if I were editing a stranger's work."

When she reads through her draft during this first revision pass, she leaves herself notes in the margins and makes a list of questions and problems. She sorts these problems by priority as she goes. For example, a character's unclear motivation is a giant problem that affects the entire manuscript, whereas a scene that needs to be set in a different location is a much smaller problem.

Rachael writes her manuscript's problems on 2x2 sticky notes as she reads through and fixes those to a sheet of paper at the front of her draft so she can see them all at a glance and prioritize them.

Resist the temptation to dive in and start solving your draft's problems just yet! Why? Because the last thing you want to do is spend days tinkering with your opening scene or a tertiary argument or a minor character's story arc only to realize you'll have to cut that entire part.

Rachael also suggested making a one-sentence outline of every scene as you read through, jotting down a few words about what happens in each scene. This document will help you move back and forth throughout the manuscript as you work out how to solve problems, and it will also help you see if your argument or story flows from beginning to end.

You may already know the solutions to some of your problems. Others may be trickier. But now that you have a giant list, you can begin to solve them.

In *The Secrets of Story,* Matt Bird offers a brilliant suggestion to help writers brainstorm solutions. Rather than looking at every item on your list as an individual problem with a single solution, start by brainstorming dozens of possible solutions to the biggest problems on your list. Once you've done that, look through your potential solutions to find the ones that will eliminate multiple problems at once. When you pair off problems, you're not only making your solutions do double duty, you're also avoiding the trap of solving problems at an individual level without really integrating them into the rest of your book.

Start Big and Go Small

Grab your list of problems, your one-sentence scene or section outline, and your "save-as" version of your manuscript. It's time to get your hands dirty.

Take your outline and ask yourself how each chapter and section flows in the larger context of the book. If you're writing nonfiction, does each chapter feel like the next step in the process, or build on the information that came before it? You might notice that there's no real transition from one concept to the next, that you're jumping around in time, or that there are logical gaps in your argument. Rearrange your outline accordingly.

In fiction, scenes basically come in two types, and most stories naturally alternate the two. "Scenes" are action-oriented as a character attempts to achieve a goal. "Sequels" are reactions, as the character regroups from and reflects on what just occurred and decides what to do next. Your pacing will feel off if you have too many action scenes in a row with no chance for a breath or too many reaction scenes that aren't actively pushing the plot forward.

Start reorganizing your draft according to your new outline. This is relatively simple to do in a program like Scrivener or Ulysses that allows you to break large text documents into individual scenes and subsections.

Then, start working through your list of problems and solutions. As a general rule, start by sorting out your big, structure-level problems before dealing with scene problems. But sometimes, Fonda pointed out, it can be hard to know exactly how to fix that big problem until you get started working. "Sometimes I start with what I know how to do first," she said. "I'll work on other things while I'm stewing on how to fix the big problems."

At this level you'll also start figuring out where to plant seeds and foreshadow payoffs for the reader. You know when you're reading a book and you gasp, realizing that the author cleverly planted hints for a fantastic payoff along the way? Some of those hints might be magical moments of the subconscious, but it's more likely the author added in hints of foreshadowing and resonance in the revision stage. This is the place where you make yourself look very smart indeed, like you knew where you were going the whole time.

Some writers like to work on an individual problem and fix it throughout the manuscript wherever it appears. For example, if you have a character arc that needs to be worked on, you might make those changes in each scene, then go through and make the next changes on your list.

I usually use the comments feature in Scrivener to make notes in the draft about things that need to be fixed. For example, if a plot point needs to be set up better, I'll brainstorm all the places that I could foreshadow it, then go back to each scene and leave a comment about what I need to do there.

Then, I work through the draft in order, knowing that I've noted everything that needs to happen in each scene from a big structural view.

And, of course, as you're working through this big picture pass on your second draft, keep your core idea or theme in mind.

Take Action

Save a new copy of your manuscript, print it out, grab your favorite beverage, and start reading through with pen in hand like you've never seen it before in your life.

- Write down your core idea somewhere it will be visible during the revision process.

- Ignore grammar and spelling errors, and leave yourself notes in the margins as you read.

- List any big problems you see in a notebook, computer file, or on Stickys.

- List out your scenes or sections, and make notes on how they flow, as well as any places where you need to foreshadow future events.

- Once you're done reading, prioritize problems from biggest to smallest and start brainstorming solutions.

- Open your saved-as version of the file and reorganize your draft according to your new outline.

- Start working through the problems from biggest to smallest.

Fixing Section-Level Problems

In your first revision pass, you were looking at big, structural problems that affected the entire book. You wrestled the big picture into some semblance of an order, and you should now have a draft that more or less makes sense.

Now it's time to start taking a closer look at how each scene or chapter works on its own.

Think of each scene and chapter as a mini story or essay within a larger work. In fiction, each scene should have a setup, conflict, and resolution—the reader should know the character's motivation and goal for this chapter and be rooting for them to succeed or fail. In nonfiction, the reader should understand the thesis, get the supporting arguments, and get a satisfying conclusion. Each chapter might work on its own as a blog post or article, while also contributing to the overall thesis of your book.

This is the most enjoyable aspect of the revision process for me, because trying to wrangle big structural stuff can feel overwhelming. I'll often still move scenes and chapters around as I'm digging into this section-level revision because I'm more immersed in the draft—and, therefore, the reader experience—at this stage. Where the structure-level revision is a bit more intellectual, section-level revision is more instinctual regarding how best to tell the story or lay out an argument.

At this stage, I'll almost always go through the book sequentially. The exception is if I'm writing a novel where one character has a storyline separate from the main narrative. For example, in book three of the Bulari Saga, I introduced a detective side character who was investigating my main characters. I ended up treating his scenes almost as their own shorter story and revising them all in one pass separate from the rest of the book.

While you should be thinking more about your prose at this point, don't spend too much time polishing sentences. There's still the danger that you might decide to cut a section or that you'll get to a later chapter and realize you need to jump back and change things. We'll make your prose gleam in the editing pass.

Fiction

Each scene in a novel should read like a story with a beginning, middle, and end. Keep in mind that a scene and a chapter aren't (necessarily) the same thing. A chapter may be made up of multiple scenes, or a single long scene may be broken up into multiple chapters. With longer, slower-paced works like epic fantasy or historical fiction, there may be three or four scenes in a long chapter. In fast-paced thrillers, chapter breaks within a single scene can keep readers turning pages.

Some fiction writers wait until they have the entire book revised to make decisions on chapter breaks, some do it as they go.

Start by taking a close look at where you begin your scene. The goal should be to bring the reader into the scene as late into the action as possible, but you may have written too much in your first draft—the real starting point may be buried. How much of the action at the beginning of the scene could you cut out and still have the scene make sense?

Note the beats of description, dialogue, action, and exposition throughout your scene. Do they build on each other to raise the stakes and tension to its own mini climax? Where are your reveals and reversals? At this stage, it can be very helpful to outline your scene, giving yourself a visual of how the action arcs.

Finally, the end of every scene and chapter should point to the next. For a masterclass in this, read Fonda Lee's *Jade City*. The final sentences of every chapter point you directly to the next chapter and make you want to know what happens next.

Don't be afraid of cliffhangers in your chapters! Readers will complain about them, but when well done it'll make you stay up until four in the morning reading the book. One excellent example of this is K.B. Wagers's Indranan War series. Wagers routinely ends chapters mid-scene at a cliffhanger moment and also breaks for scenes in the middle of a chapter. Because readers tend to want to read "just one more chapter," the technique makes these books incredibly hard to put down.

Nonfiction

Nonfiction chapters should also have a narrative arc to them: introduce the chapter's subject, lay out your argument, then sum it up at the end. As Robert, who gives a lot of sales presentations, likes to say, a good presentation (and a good chapter) has three parts: tell them what you're going to tell them, tell them, and tell them what you told them.

As you revise each chapter, make sure everything you include is aligned with the subject of that chapter. Are there any facts, anecdotes, or stories that would be a better fit in a different chapter? Are you repeating anything you wrote elsewhere? Are there any lines or sections you're holding onto that don't actually serve the story?

At this stage, you're really shaping the book for your reader. Put yourself in their shoes and ask: What do they need to know about this topic? What other questions might they have? If you didn't have any knowledge of this subject, would you be able to follow your own argument in this chapter?

As with fiction, you want to end each section with a hook that piques your reader's curiosity and points them to the next chapter. One way to do this is by giving them a taste of what you'll be talking about in the next chapter and explaining the value the reader will get out of it. Another option is to pose a teaser question that makes them want to read on: "And why on earth do pangolins need such a long tongue? As you'll find out in the next chapter, the truth is stranger than you could expect."

Take Action

Work through each subsection of your book, asking the following questions as you go:

For each fiction scene, ask yourself:

- How does this scene advance the plot, character, and conflict?

- Does this scene have a mini arc of setup, conflict, and resolution?

- Does the scene start at the right place?

- Does the reader know what your characters want going into each scene, and whether they succeeded or failed at the end? Is it clear what success or failure means to the rest of the story?

- Is the scene making the emotional impact on the characters—and readers—that you intend it to?

- Is there enough sensory detail to draw the reader into the scene?

- Is everything in the scene necessary? How could cutting material improve the scene?

- Is your dialogue clear? Does it drive the story forward?

- Does the scene end with a hook or cliffhanger that makes the reader want to turn the page?

For each nonfiction chapter, ask yourself:

- Does this chapter answer the question it poses and tie into the overall topic?

- Is there a beginning, middle, and end? (Tell them what you're going to tell them, tell them, tell them what you told them.)

- Does this chapter naturally build on the previous chapter?

- Is the topic clear and the argument well-supported with enough examples, facts, and anecdotes?

- Are you skipping any important steps or missing any transitions?

- Are you making your point as succinctly as possible without being repetitive or getting off topic?

- Is there anything you can cut to improve the reader's experience?

- Does the end of this chapter make your reader want to turn the page to read the next chapter?

Polishing Your Prose

You've got a draft that makes sense, both structurally and at the section level. Congratulations, that's huge! (Ayelet Weisz would ask you what you're doing to celebrate.) It's time for one more pass before you send it off to your beta readers, your writing group, your editor—whoever you are next trusting with your work.

In this pass, you're polishing up your prose as much as you can before the professional editor takes your good work into excellent territory. (More on that in a minute.)

Writers tend to either love editing or hate it. Maybe you're so sick of your book by this point, you can't stand the idea of reading it again. In that case, I recommend taking a break for a bit and working on something else to clear your brain—especially if you've done some major surgery on your previous versions of the manuscript. Let the dust settle, let yourself get excited about the project again, and dive back in.

I actually love editing. It's one of my favorite parts, because it's where the book feels like it's reaching the ideal that I had in my head. The muddy theses become razor-sharp, the jokes land, the characters feel real, the dialogue is snappy. This is also where I can waste a lot of time going over and over a scene, tweaking words and digging for gold.

(If that's you, remind yourself that your goal here is "good enough." Your draft will still go to an editor, and you'll get that final chance to polish before it heads out in the world!)

It's a good idea to print out your manuscript again at this point because it's easier to catch errors when you're looking at it in a different way. If you do edit on your computer, try changing the font to help trick your brain into catching mistakes you might otherwise gloss over.

I edit on my computer, but for my final proofreading pass, I'll often load the manuscript on my e-reader, because it's a different reading experience than on the computer. I use the highlight feature to note any typos or other errors—which I always find, even after multiple passes by myself and my editor.

Take Action

- Keep an eye out for basic grammar: Do a quick reread of *The Elements of Style* by William Strunk Jr. and E.B. White, and keep it in mind as you do your self-editing pass. Tools such as Grammarly or Hemingway Editor can be fantastic for helping flag grammar errors, too.

- Watch for passive sentences: One of my favorites I caught recently: "There was a bench near the door for Phaera to sit on." —> "Phaera sat on the bench beside the door." Rewrite passive sentences to make them more engaging and less wordy.

- Keep it simple!: Big words are fun, but simpler is usually better when it comes to getting your point across and engaging the reader. Ask yourself, is there a simpler way to say something? A simpler word to use? George Orwell's six rules for writing include this one for a reason: "Never use a long word where a short one will do."

- Avoid repetition: Sometimes it takes a few tries to say something right—but too often those earlier attempts are left on the page. Are you restating the same idea multiple times in a paragraph or chapter? Figure out which is the best and cut the rest.

- Watch for "throat clearing": In fiction, are your characters on stage a few minutes before the meat of the scene starts? In nonfiction, do you have needless preambles and asides before you give the reader the juicy information they're there for? As writers, we sometimes spend too many words clearing our proverbial throats in order to get to the point. Cut it.

- Search for overused words: I keep a list of words that I know I overuse in my fiction including: shrug, breath, eyebrow, only, just, look, frown, see, and glance. Some of these are words I've recognized, some are words my editor has pointed out to me. When I've finished my polishing pass on every chapter, I go through and search for all the words on my list.

- Cut your draft by 10 percent: *The 10% Solution: Self-Editing for the Modern Writer* by Ken Rand is a fantastic short book detailing one simple self-editing trick: why you should aim to cut every draft by 10 percent and how to do it. Similar to my list of overused words, Rand has a list of words and syllables that indicate problems such as wordiness, passive sentences, and pompousness. These include: -ly, of, very, that, -ion, -ing, and was. Searching your manuscript for these words and rewriting the offending sentences tightens up your prose.

- Pay attention to visuals: The way the text looks on the page influences the reader's experience. A giant wall of text feels dense and claustrophobic (which is why Gabriel García Márquez chose to write *The Autumn of the Patriarch*, a story about a dictator trapped in the confines of his home and mind, without any paragraph breaks). On the other hand, you'll notice many fast-paced thriller novels are full of short paragraphs that make your eyes speed down the page. Play with how your text appears on the page to influence the reading experience.

- Read your work aloud: When you read a piece silently on the screen (or on paper), your brain will fill in missing words. Reading your work aloud can help you catch errors and also point out clunky sentences. You can also use your computer's screen reading software to read your book to you.

- Vary sentences: Note if you have a bunch of sentences in a row that are a similar length or have a similar construction.

Even if readers don't consciously realize that's what's happening, static sentence structures can make your prose feel stilted or off-kilter. (Reading your work aloud is a great tool to help you catch those!) Also pay attention to sentence beginnings to ensure you're not starting off too many sentences in the same way.

- BONUS! Take an improvement pass: I got this idea from editor Bonnie Johnston when she presented on developmental editing at the StoryShop Summit in 2020. After the editing pass, she does a final improvement pass where she picks one craft element she wants to practice, then spends five minutes per scene fixing one instance. For example, you might choose to make descriptions more active, deepen character emotion, make dialogue snappier, or include sensory details. The improvement pass helps drill that craft element into your head and is a great way to learn and level up for the next book you write.

N ow you have a draft that's as polished as you can make it on your own. It's time to bring in outside eyes to help you get it across the finish line. Let's talk about who some of those people might be.

Critique Partners

Critique partners are generally a formalized relationship where you meet together regularly (or for a longer one-time workshop) to critique each person in the group's work. Critique partners will almost always be other writers.

Early on in my career, I went through a series of writing critique groups with other writers who were at a similar place in their writing journey. (Unpublished, still learning our craft.) The longest running was in Seattle. It consisted of me and three other writers who had met at a local science fiction and fantasy writer's convention. We called ourselves the Shining Creamsicles.

Our format was simple: We met once a month at one member's house. We'd chat about writing and life over dinner, then we would take our drinks to the living room and critique whoever's work we were reading that month. Normally it would be a short story or a few chapters; we'd rotate through the crew so that each of us got a chance to have work critiqued a few times a year, but we didn't have the pressure of being under the spotlight every month.

After the Shining Creamsicles eventually dissolved (life and travels scattered us across the globe), a friend and I wrangled together another critique circle, this one with the express purpose of all of us finishing our first novels. The format was similar (dinner and drinks are a must for me when it comes to critique circles), but we met quarterly. Each quarter, all four of the group's members would submit a quarter of our novels-in-progress, and we'd critique all four submissions in one (long) sitting. Then we all went back home to write the next quarter.

This type of group can be incredibly helpful in the early years of your writing career. Critiquing others' writing can be just as valuable as having your own critiqued, as it requires you to articulate why a piece doesn't grab your attention, why a description falls flat, why a character doesn't ring true. When you can articulate that about someone else's work, it's easier to see that in your own.

To find this kind of group, go to writers conferences, join local write-ins and writer social events, and start asking others if they're interested. If it's not a great fit, it's better to move on than to let a bad writer's group drain the life out of your writing.

You also might find a formal group in your area, or join a critique circle.

Writers who seek out a formalized education will probably find critique partners in their undergrad or MFA program. (The novel-writing group was made up of friends I'd met in college.) But many long-going critique groups will sometimes advertise for new members. When we moved to Portland, I was briefly in a regular critique group that I found through Craigslist.

Beta Readers

Beta readers are incredible, wonderful folks who will read your (mostly) finished draft or sections of your piece as you go along. They can be other writers, but they don't have to be. You may have a semi-formal relationship with them, or it may be more casual.

Eventually, I moved away from critique circles, in part because I felt like I had a stronger sense of my own writing, and in part because I was working at a much faster pace than these sorts of circles tend to.

Instead, I started sending my work to individual beta readers to get feedback. Most of these were writers I knew, and we would trade beta reads of each other's novels.

A beta read is a bit different than a critique, in that it's more about taking off your writer hat and putting on a reader hat. As a beta reader, you're asking yourself, does the story work? Does this argument make sense? Is this section boring? Did I get confused?

While critique partners will almost always be other writers, your beta readers can be a mix of writers and readers. You want to find people who understand your genre, whether you're writing thrillers or self-help. At this stage, you're trying to take your rough draft and craft it into something that appeals to your ideal reader, so you want beta readers who fall into that category. Giving your romance novel draft to a friend who only reads military science fiction probably won't get you helpful feedback.

One of my longest and best beta readers is a college friend who's a knitting pattern designer. She's not a writer, but she loves to read, and she's fantastic at pointing out where she got lost in the plot, when character actions aren't believable, and whether or not she's satisfied by the ending. She's also one of my ideal readers, so I know if she's happy with the book, others will be.

You may start to collect a circle of beta readers who are good at different parts of the process.

Some may be whizzes at structure and the big picture, which means you might want to send them an earlier draft where you're still trying to get the bones of your plot in place, or the main idea of your nonfiction book.

Some may be amazing at language, character motivation, and nuance. You might want to send them a later draft, when the bones of the piece are more solid, so they can exercise their skills without getting caught up in the fact that there's still something off, structurally.

And, as you collect beta readers, you might accidentally net a special one.

You might catch an alpha reader.

Alpha Readers

Alpha readers are rare, magical creatures who you can trust with the raw, messy stuff that will someday become a real draft. Your prose won't be perfect, your ideas might be still half-formed. Sharing this early, delicate work with someone who doesn't respect what you're allowing them to read can be damaging to a writer's psyche, so be sure your alpha reader is worthy of your trust.

I found my alpha reader when I wrote the first book of the Bulari Saga, *Double Edged*.

Well, I guess I found him almost a decade before that, when I walked into his studio apartment with a keg of beer for the party. But until I finished writing *Double Edged*, I'd been too nervous to let Robert read much of my writing.

Over the years I'd slowly let him read some stories, and he'd read some early drafts of novels that came before *Double Edged*. He'd given me a bit of feedback on a few of the Bulari Saga prequel novellas, which I wrote as I was trying to get a handle on story structure and backstory.

Robert isn't a writer, but he reads a ton, and he has a great sense of story structure and what makes things work. He's also a harsh critic. He has high standards, and he wants to see only my best work out there in the world.

In the past I'd only given him permission to give me vague direction if something wasn't working, but with *Double Edged* I gave him permission to tear the draft to shreds.

I printed out the entire manuscript. He spent a week reading it with a frown and a pen in hand. My heart kicked into high-anxiety mode every time I saw him working. (And I eventually had to forbid him from reading it around me because it was so nerve-wracking.)

When he was done, it took us the entirety of a weekend and several bottles of wine to get through his notes on the draft. I cried. We fought. I took notes. We busted out board game figurines and blocked the final battle scene on the dining room table. I cried some more.

And then, mentally exhausted and overwhelmed by the experience, I wrote the next draft of *Double Edged*.

It was a billion times better than it had been before.

I've started involving Robert earlier and earlier in the process, and now we hold regular story meetings as I write. I give him my outline before I start writing, then I print out each quarter of the book for him to tear apart as I go. I then revise that quarter before writing the next quarter.

He's gone from someone I was terrified to share my work with to a vital part of my writing process because I know that I can trust him with the rawest, earliest forms of my ideas.

Since that first meeting, he's learned to be gentler with his feedback, and I've learned to take it more gracefully. But it's still emotional work to let someone read my unfinished work before I've had a chance to lacquer it up and protect it.

If you can find an alpha reader, you've found an incredible gift.

Tips for Working with Early Readers

If you have five people read your work, you'll likely get eight different opinions and a dozen conflicting ideas about how to fix it.

The *reactions* of your readers are the most useful thing to know. Did they love a part? Where were they confused? Were they surprised? (In a good way? A bad way?) Where did they get bored? What bumped them out of the story or annoyed them?

"How to fix it" bits of advice generally aren't helpful. When you're working with a critique group of other writers, they may offer you diagnoses and prescriptions. Take diagnoses with a grain of salt and—generally—ignore prescriptions entirely. Another writer may have advice for how to fix a character motivation or fuzzy argument, but you're the only one who knows for sure how to make your book work.

For new writers especially, it can be a temptation to either try to address all feedback or ignore it all. But even if you disagree with the feedback—or your readers disagree with each other—it can be a valuable temperature check for how things are going in your draft.

When you're looking at the feedback, try to get some distance so it's not so stressful. After all, you just asked someone to give you their honest reactions to something that's personal, close to your heart. Don't respond or start changing things right away— take some time to let it sink in and get through your emotional defenses.

It's okay to ask for clarification if you don't understand why an early reader had a problem with something, and it's okay to decide that they're wrong. They might have different tastes, likes, and dislikes. They might bounce off your main character because she reminds them of a hated coworker. They also might not be a good reader for you—for example, if you're writing a romantic suspense novel and they mostly read epic historical fiction, they may critique your work based on the genre conventions they're familiar with, rather than the ones you should be paying attention to. Or maybe they tend to prefer pop science books when you're writing for an academic audience.

But before you decide your early reader is wrong, try to see if there really is an issue. It might not be the one they pointed out, but their reaction could be a symptom of a problem. (If multiple readers stumbled on the same thing, this is definitely the case.)

When I disagree with a critique, I often find that the problem isn't with the thing they mentioned, but with the way I'm communicating it. If Robert doesn't think an action is in character but I strongly feel that it is, I'm not communicating that character correctly to him as a reader. I'll ask him why he thinks that action is out of character and try to track down the root of the perception issue.

While reader feedback is helpful, don't let this become writing a book by committee. Fonda Lee, who generally has multiple early readers for every book she writes, recommended viewing all the feedback through your vision. "You ideally need some sense of confidence and vision in your own work," she told me. "That way you can filter all the advice that you get from beta readers through the lens of asking, 'Does this get me closer to my vision or not?'"

Take Action

Find someone to give you feedback on your draft. Remember, you wrote this first of all with yourself in mind, but now it's time to let your ideal readers into the room.

It may take some time to collect the right early readers for your work, but if you keep at it, you'll find getting feedback on your work to be incredibly rewarding.

Here are some ideas for finding early readers:

- Attend a local writing conference in your area and connect with like-minded writers at a similar stage of their career.

- Post an ad for critique partners on your local Craigslist, or leave a flyer in your favorite coffee shop.

- Search for a critique group on Meetup.org (or a write-in group, where you don't do critiques but you may meet people who could be good critique partners.

- Join an online critique group through Critique.org.

- Form your own online critique group by searching out writers in your genre through social media groups and hashtags.

- Ask a friend you trust to read an early draft, and ask them to use author Mary Robinette Kowal's *ABCD*s of critiquing. The reader simply notes *A* for awesome, *B* for boring, *C* for confusing, or *D* for disbelief.

Working with an Editor

At some point, you'll have gotten your work as good as you can on your own, and with the help of your early readers. It's time to involve the professionals. If you're working with an agent and/ or publisher, their editing team will lead the charge. If you're publishing the work yourself, you can hire your own editor.

Working with a great editor is an enormous blessing, because they can make your work magical. They're trained to polish prose, yes, but they can also catch errors and make suggestions that you're too close to the text to see. A great editor understands your voice and goals for the project, and challenges you to be your best.

In my freelance career, I've been lucky enough to work with an ex-newspaper editor for several years, writing content marketing articles for higher ed companies. He doesn't let any lazy writing or reporting get past him, which has forced me to up my game and grow as a writer. The editor I work with on all my fiction books, Kyra Freestar, knows my voice so well that she'll sometimes rewrite clunky sentences entirely for me, and they always sound as if I wrote them at my best.

Let's talk about finding the right editor and creating a fruitful relationship.

A Field Guide to Editors

Editors come with a range of specializations, and you might work with several at different stages in the process.

Drafting Stage

First, there are editors who will help you in the drafting process to develop your idea and give feedback on the draft as you work on it. This is generally a hands-off process, in that you're receiving feedback and implementing it yourself, rather than the editor actually making changes to the draft.

- Developmental edit/editorial critique/editorial review: A developmental editor will help you with the overall structure and big picture of your piece. This type of editor might also be known as a book doctor or manuscript consultant.

- Sensitivity edit: A sensitivity editor or sensitivity reader is someone with lived experience in a culture or identity you're not familiar with, who can help you make sure you're providing an accurate representation in your book. You might also hire this type of subject matter expert to give feedback on your use of unfamiliar technology, science, military jargon, etc.

Polishing Stage

At some point, you're done drafting and ready to polish the manuscript. Then, any editor you're working with will be actively editing your draft. They'll be fixing sentences and catching high-level errors, rather than looking at big-picture things like structure or character arcs.

Line edit: A line editor concentrates on your sentences and how those sentences build into paragraphs. This edit focuses on language and style—clarity, tone, redundancies, and flow.

Copy edit: This is the final polish work on your manuscript; you won't be making any substantial changes to the piece at this point. A good copy editor catches typos and grammatical errors, as well as leveling up your prose and tracking for spelling and grammatical consistency and factual errors. For my fiction, Kyra also copy edits for continuity—no easy task on a series that has eight books.

Proofread: No matter how many passes your work has gone through, there will always be typos. Always factor proofreading into your time and budget. For my fiction, I do a proofreading pass, as well as sending it to advanced readers before publication. We always catch at least a handful of typos, like the fact that I'd misspelled my main character's name on the very last page of one novel.

Keep in mind that an individual editor may do multiple types of editing, but they can't do it all at the same time. For example, a developmental editor probably won't also copy edit your manuscript, because you're still revising. Along the same lines, a line editor won't generally give you notes on structure or character arcs, because the assumption is that the story is complete as is and they're putting the finishing touches on the prose.

At times Kyra will suggest bigger-picture edits (such as tightening up a character's motivation or, in one case, writing a denouement scene to give the reader a more satisfying conclusion). But the line editing stage isn't the place to see if a character arc is working. That should have been taken care of in an earlier editing pass.

Also, keep in mind that your manuscript won't be "done" once a copy or line editor goes through it. You'll still need to go through all their edits and make sure you agree with them, or rework sections that are unclear. Depending on the scope of the edits, this can take a few more days or even weeks of work.

Hiring the Right Editor

As I said above, if you have a contract with a traditional publisher, they'll provide an editor for you. You'll want to edit the manuscript to the best of your own ability before turning it in, but you don't need to hire your own editor first.

But if you're self-publishing, take the time to shop around and find the person who will be the perfect fit for you.

Kyra noted this means making sure they have the skill set you're looking for, as well as whether their personality is a good match.

"It does matter who you're working with," Kyra told me. "I don't even mean personality, but are you able to easily communicate with them?"

Start by interviewing multiple editors to find the person you feel most comfortable with and feel the most confident about. Ask other writers in your genre who they have used, or check the acknowledgements section of other indie authors' books to see if they shout-out to their editor.

Some editors may have questionnaires and information on their website about their approach, others may prefer to get on the phone and talk with you to get a sense of your project. But whether by phone or by email, pay attention to how easily you can communicate, Kyra said. "Pick the one you feel most comfortable with and confident about after you've talked to them."

Not only do you need to make sure you're both on the same page about what type of editing they'll do (make sure your definitions of line editing match, for example), you also want to work with someone who is a good fit for your genre and style. For example, Kyra gets my sense of humor and the tone of the world of my novels. Someone who didn't mesh with me like that might end up flattening the quirks of my prose rather than polishing them to gleaming.

Editors are also trying to find a good fit, so don't be shy about telling them that you're shopping around. Many editors will offer to do a sample edit of a few pages so you can get a sense of how they will edit your prose. That can help you determine if they're going to gel with your style, or if their edits won't work for you.

Working with Editors

Every time I get edits back—whether it's for an article or a novel—I break out into a cold sweat. Even with the last book of the Bulari Saga, having gone through this process eight times before with Kyra, I opened her editorial letter with a spike of fear.

Rachael Herron likes to tell new writers that getting a revision letter is like being in a blast zone, and for three or four days you may feel the shock. That's normal. You just handed your precious work off to a professional for evaluation, and they gave it back with proverbial red ink all over it.

It's going to be fine.

Let your emotions settle for a couple of hours or days, then take another look. When you give yourself time to let your defenses down, you'll start to make sense of the revision letter, piece by piece. The enormity of the edits you need to tackle will start to seem more manageable.

Rachael had gotten her twenty-seventh revision letter the week I interviewed her. "I don't think that feeling ever goes away," she told me. "I knew she was right, but I didn't know how to do what she wanted me to. I figured it was impossible! And then two days later, I started to think, maybe I *can* do this."

So just be ready for that shock, know that it'll be fine, take a deep breath, and dive in.

The Editorial Letter

Most editors will send you a large letter detailing everything that's awful about your book.

I'm kind of kidding. But the letter *will* point out the big-picture issues they spotted while going through your manuscript and some potential solutions. (And hopefully some of the things they loved, too!)

For nonfiction books, an editor may push back on unsubstantiated claims or arguments that aren't developed enough. They'll take the place of the reader and ask questions you overlooked or point to gaps in your logic. With fiction, an editor may note continuity issues, inconsistencies in how your characters act, motivations, gaps in world-building, or the next logical step in the plot. The editorial letter may also contain less soul-shattering feedback like lists of words you overused.

You may agree wholeheartedly with some of the points. Others, not so much. If you don't agree with something, let it sit a while before responding to see if, like Rachael noted, it starts to make sense to you. If it still doesn't make sense, it's always okay to ask for clarification.

And if you firmly disagree, it's also okay to push back!

When I asked Kyra what writers need to know about the editorial process, she noted that all edits are suggestions, and authors should feel free to push back. At the same time, editors generally have educated and experienced suggestions, and so instead of outright dismissing an edit you disagree with, try to figure out if there's a misunderstanding.

"My goal is to support the work," said Kyra. "If I do misstep with an edit, that means I misunderstood what your goal was with that sentence or word or paragraph. The suggestion may be wrong, but it means there's something to work on in terms of getting the correct message or feeling across."

Line Edits and Copy Edits

If you're working with a developmental editor, you may only get an editorial letter. Otherwise, you'll also get your manuscript back with tracked changes (visible, in-line suggested edits) and comments.

At this stage, I start a revision checklist. I jot down all the big-picture items to keep in mind from the editorial letter, along with any other things I may have decided to change during the time my editor had the manuscript. I also add the latest batch of overused words to my master list of "words to search for" that I use in the self-editing stage.

Then, I take a deep breath and open up the manuscript. I work in tracked changes from page one to the end, reading every word and noting the editor's copy edits and either leaving them alone or "stetting" them, which means telling the editor to leave the original as is. With editors I've worked with regularly, I rarely disagree with their edits.

I also address any comments as I go. Sometimes the comments are easy fixes, but other times they're a thorny mess that require a nice walk around the neighborhood and some time mulling about in my brain before I can tackle them. I will rarely move on until I've solved that particular problem, but it's also okay to mark it and come back to it later if it needs more time to marinate.

When I finally reach the end, I double check my revision checklist to make sure I got everything. Then, I return the manuscript with my own tracked changes to the editor for a cleanup pass and treat myself to a well-earned sushi dinner.

PART FOUR

WHAT'S NEXT?

"Art is never finished, only abandoned." –Leonardo da Vinci

W hat do you do now that you've written the thing?

I hinted at this in the beginning, but I want to reiterate: Writing can be a great way to get your ideas out in the world or a private way to process your thoughts. It can earn you a living, or it can be a hobby you enjoy and want to get better at. There's no one *right* way to be a writer, just as there's no one right writing process.

You can't control the outcome of what you've written, but you can improve your craft and build a writing process you enjoy. One that energizes and fulfills you when you sit down at your desk, rather than stressing you out or making you feel like you're doing things wrong.

Whatever your reasons for writing, you've finished a thing. And that means celebrating!

Charlie Gilkey calls this running a victory lap in *Start Finishing*. Celebrating can seem selfish, Charlie writes, but it's not just about you. "What we so often forget, though, is that the victory lap isn't just about the victor but also the community." People in your lives, your writing community, your family, they've been cheering you on. They've been hearing you talk about this book. They've been inspired by you. In one way or another, they've been instrumental in helping you accomplish your goal. Acknowledge that and give them a chance to celebrate you.

Tell your friends and family what you've finished. Train yourself to answer, "How's it going?" with "I finished my book!!!" It's a momentous accomplishment, one that few people will actually do.

The hard thing about celebrating the end of a writing project is that it never quite feels "done." I used to struggle with when to allow myself to celebrate a project. Was it when I finished the first draft? When I turned it in to the editor? When it was finally published? When it had sold enough copies for me to feel like I was a "real writer?" But then I remember my friend, Ayelet Weisz, quick to remind me that each step is worth celebrating!

Since I was a kid, I admired my grandmother's opal ring, and I wanted one of my own. When I was working on my first published novel, I promised myself I would buy an opal ring when it was published—but when the time came, I didn't do it. It was just a micropress publication, I told myself. It wasn't that big of a deal. I had other books I was working on. Who did I think I was, anyway?

For *years* I would occasionally browse Etsy looking at opal rings, telling myself that I would buy one when I finished the next book. But the next book was *just* a novella. And the book after that was somehow also just as inconsequential.

It wasn't until I finished the first book of the Bulari Saga (my fifth published book) that I mentioned this to Robert. He looked at me like I was an alien. "How many more books do you need to finish before you can buy yourself a gift for finishing your first book?"

I bought myself a ring.

It has four opals in it—partly because it's the one I loved, but partly as a reminder to myself that I waited four books too long to celebrate that first big accomplishment.

So let me be your cheerleader: Go! Celebrate! Allow yourself to be excited and happy and proud, even though there's more work on the horizon. Allow your community the opportunity to join in by sharing the good news.

My point is that it's important to celebrate your wins, no matter how much work there seems to be left. Writing is a lifetime journey, so build a ritual around your wins, whether that's a trip to your favorite spendy restaurant, a pair of shoes, or just buying yourself a slice of cake from the bakery.

You put in a whole lot of work, and you're worth it.

PUT IT OUT THERE

You write for those people whose lives you might touch. That person who needs to hear your story, who will read it and feel seen. Who will become inspired. Who will find a sense of healing. Who will enjoy a moment's distraction then close your book and return to their life reinvigorated and refreshed and ready to give it their all.

You may hear from these people, or you may not. But either way, when you drop your story like a pebble in a lake, the ripples will flow out.

But you have to drop it into that lake.

What it means to put it out there is different for every person. Especially these days when there are so many options for you to publish your work and find an audience. The route you choose will depend on your goals and personality, but the important thing is getting your work in front of readers. Even if you're just doing like my grandmother did with the manuscript of her early memories: printing out a handful of copies and distributing them to family members in three-ring binders at Christmas.

Putting your writing in front of a reader completes the cycle, and transforms it from a private act to an act of community. But it also pushes you forward as a writer.

"It's hard to improve your writing if you're just writing for yourself," Charlie told me. "If you're serious about improving your craft as a writer, if you're serious about improving your voice and figuring out what you actually think, you need to publish."

How to get published is outside the scope of this particular book, but there are two broad routes available to writers today.

Traditional Route

Find a publisher. Whether you're looking to place essays in a magazine or have a novel you'd love to see in bookstores, narrow down a list of publishers you would like to work with and figure out how to get your manuscript in front of them.

Many magazines and newspapers take cold pitches, as do some small press publishers. The bigger ones generally only look at agented submissions, which means that for most authors heading down the traditional path means starting by finding an agent.

A traditional publisher will take care of the production process for you, editing your book, designing the cover, and distributing it. You'll still have to do the work of getting your book in front of the audience, but the traditional route can open audiences that would be difficult to reach on your own.

Self-Publishing Route

Become your own publisher. Start a blog or an account on a site like Medium, and post your essays there. Publish your books directly as e-books through the major online distributors, and have paperbacks available through print-on-demand services.

When you go this route, you'll need to take care of the production process, including hiring an editor and cover designer, producing the book itself, and handling the distribution. You're also in charge of the marketing and publicity—literally every aspect is under your control. (And your responsibility.)

It's still possible to get a wide audience and even get your book into bookstores. But it takes a lot more energy than with a traditional publisher.

Which Should You Choose?

If you like running your own business, like me, going the self-publishing route might sound appealing. If you'd rather spend your precious writing time on writing rather than learning how to format books, you might prefer the traditional route.

If you just want to get your memoirs in front of a few people, self-publishing is a great way to go. If you want to win the Caldecott Medal for your children's picture book, you're going to need to go traditional.

As with writing, there's no "right" way—just what works best for you.

Find Community

Curtis Chen is the person who introduced me to most of the writers I've met in Portland, mostly through the write-ins and Science Fiction and Fantasy Writers of America happy hours he hosts. He does such a fantastic job of bringing people together in the sci-fi and fantasy community that I wasn't surprised by his answer when I asked for the biggest piece of advice he had for newer writers: Community.

"Finding a community that works for you will sustain you through a lot of the ups and downs," said Curtis. "We all go through very similar things with our creative projects, so having people to talk with is important."

I second that.

Writing is by nature a solitary activity, but it doesn't have to be. If the idea of putting yourself out there to meet other writers is intimidating, remember that most writers are shy and introverted and, like you, just want to meet new people. It took me years to learn that most people aren't being standoffish—they're just too shy to take the initiative, and they'll be grateful if you get up the courage to say hello.

Here are some places to meet other writers who may become potential friends, collaborators, and early readers:

- Writing together: Look for in-person write-ins in your area or virtual ones worldwide through sites like Meetup.com. Many of these will have a specific format (such as write for twenty-five minutes, chat for ten minutes) that helps you get work done while also giving a chance to get to know the other participants.

- Conferences: Writing conferences are another great way to connect with other writers. Many will have hands-on workshops and other ways to get feedback on your writing as well as mixers to help you meet new people. These days, a lot of conferences have gone online or have an online component, which makes them more accessible.

- Classes and workshops: Check out your local community college to see if they offer writing classes to the public, or see if a local organization offers classes. Again, you'll find a lot of great virtual classes too.

- Social media groups: You can find writing communities in Facebook Groups, Slack, Discord, and more. These can be a bit trickier to find, but as you start meeting new people, ask them where they're hanging out online and how you can get involved.

And Finally . . .

As I was finishing edits on this book, I confided to my friend Mark Teppo that I was worried about whether or not I'd written a useful enough book.

"Did you at least give them the secret of writing?" he asked.

I told him I ended it with the following advice, and he nodded.

"Yep," he said. "You spilled the secret."

The secret is this: *write the next thing.*

So you've finished your short story, your essay, your self-help book, your novel.

That's fantastic.

What are you writing next?

The journey of a writer always reminds me of this quote about cycling by Tour de France winner Greg LeMond: "It never gets easier, you just get faster." The more you practice, the bigger challenges you'll try to tackle. The more you ride, the farther you'll push yourself. The more you learn about craft, the more you'll realize there's a whole world of craft out there to learn.

Some parts of the writing process will get easier the more you do it, but you'll also take on new challenges as you improve your craft and push yourself to be a better and better writer.

But you'll never get there if you're not writing—so put down this book and get started.

May your writing bring you joy.

RESOURCES

Books on Writing

Mindset

- *The Successful Author Mindset: A Handbook for Surviving the Writer's Journey* by Joanna Penn

- *Dear Writer, You Need to Quit* by Becca Syme

- *Flow: The Psychology of Optimal Experience* by Mihaly Csikszentmihalyi

- *Bird by Bird: Some Instructions on Writing and Life* by Anne Lamott

- *Steering the Craft: A Twenty-First-Century Guide to Sailing the Sea of Story* by Ursula K. LeGuin

- *The Creative Habit: Learn It and Use It for Life* by Twyla Tharp

- *Zen in the Art of Writing* by Ray Bradbury

- *On Writing: A Memoir of the Craft* by Stephen King

- *War of Art: Break through the Blocks and Win Your Inner Creative Battles* and *Turning Pro: Tap Your Inner Power and Create Your Life's Work* by Steven Pressfield

- *Better Than Before: Mastering the Habits of Our Everyday Lives* by Gretchen Rubin

- *The Artist's Way: A Spiritual Path to Higher Creativity* by Julia Cameron

- *The Art of War For Writers: Fiction Writing Strategies, Tactics, and Exercises* by James Scott Bell

- *From Chaos to Creativity: Building a Productivity System for Artists and Writers* by Jessie Kwak

Planning

- *Endless Ideas: Master Bottomless Creativity* by Neeve Silver and Sean Platt

- *Steal Like an Artist: 10 Things Nobody Told You about Being Creative* by Austin Kleon

- *Bored and Brilliant: How Spacing Out Can Unlock Your Most Productive and Creative Self* by Manoush Zomorodi

- *The MacGyver Secret: Connect to Your Inner MacGyver and Solve Anything* by Lee David Zlotoff and Colleen Seifert, PhD

- *Wonderbook: The Illustrated Guide to Creating Imaginative Fiction* by Jeff Vandermeer

- *Writing the Other: A Practical Approach* by Nisi Shawl and Cynthia Ward

Story Structure

- *The Anatomy of Story: 22 Steps to Becoming a Master Storyteller* by John Truby

- *Wired for Story: The Writer's Guide to Using Brain Science to Hook Readers from the Very First Sentence* and *Story Genius: How to Use Brain Science to Go beyond Outlining and Write a Riveting Novel* by Lisa Cron

- *The Story Grid: What Good Editors Know* by Sean Coyne

- *Plot & Structure: Techniques and Exercises for Crafting a Plot That Grips Readers from Start to Finish* and *Write Your Novel from the Middle: A New Approach for Plotters, Pantsers, and Everyone in Between* by James Scott Bell

- *Save the Cat!: The Last Book on Screenwriting That You'll Ever Need* by Blake Snyder

- *Take off Your Pants!: Outline Your Books for Faster, Better Writing* by Libbie Hawker

- *Million Dollar Outlines* by David Farland

- *Story Structure . . . Demystified* and *Story Engineering: Mastering the 6 Core Competencies of Successful Writing* and *Story Physics: Harnessing the Underlying Forces of Storytelling* by Larry Brooks

- *Outlining Your Novel: Map Your Way to Success* by K.M. Weiland

- *Fool Proof Outline: A No-Nonsense System for Productive Brainstorming, Outlining, & Drafting Novels* by Christopher Downing

- *The Secrets of Story: Innovative Tools for Perfecting Your Fiction and Captivating Readers* by Matt Bird

- *Writing Into the Dark: How to Write a Novel Without an Outline* by Dean Wesley Smith

- *You're Gonna Need a Bigger Story: The 21st Century Survival Guide to Not Just Telling Stories, but Building Super Stories* by Houston Howard

- *Writing the Breakout Novel: Insider Advice to Taking Your Fiction to the Next Level* by Donald Maass

- *The First Five Pages: A Writer's Guide to Staying Out of the Rejection Pile* by Noah Lukeman

- *Creating Short Fiction: The Classic Guide to Writing Short Fiction* by Damon Knight

- *Hooked: Write Fiction That Grabs Readers at Page One & Never Lets Them Go* by Les Edgerton

- *The Novel Writer's Toolkit: From Idea to Bestseller* by Bob Mayer

Doing the Work

- *Start Finishing: How to Go from Idea to Done* by Charlie Gilkey

- *Finish Your Novel!: A Writer Productivity Guide* by Mark Teppo

- *Million Dollar Productivity* by Kevin J. Anderson

- *Fast-Draft Your Memoir: Write Your Life Story in 45 Hours* by Rachael Herron

Revision

- *Revision and Self-Editing for Publication: Techniques for Transforming Your First Draft into a Novel That Sells* by James Scott Bell

- *Self-Editing for Fiction Writers: How to Edit Yourself into Print* by Renni Brown and Dave King

- *Style: Toward Clarity and Grace* by Joseph M. Williams

- *The Elements of Style* by William Strunk Jr. and E.B. White

- *The 10% Solution: Self-Editing for the Modern Writer* by Ken Rand

- *Revising Fiction: A Handbook for Writers* by David Madden

Writing Podcasts

- *The Creative Penn* with Joanna Penn
- *How Do You Write* with Rachael Herron
- *The Productive Flourishing Podcast* with Charlie Gilkey and Angela Wheeler
- *Writing Excuses* with Mary Robinette Kowal, James L. Sutter, Dan Wells, Cassandra Khaw, and Howard Tayler
- *The Writer Files: Writing, Productivity, Creativity, and Neuroscience* with Kelton Reid
- *Grammar Girl* with Mignon Fogarty
- *The Prolific Writer* with Ryan J. Pelton
- *DIY MFA* with Gabriela Pereira
- *A Way with Words* with Martha Barnette and Grant Barrett
- *The Creative Writer's Toolbelt* with Andrew J Chamberlain
- *Story Grid Podcast* with Shawn Coyne and Tim Grahl
- *Write Away* with Crys Cain and JP Rindfleisch
- *You Are a Storyteller Podcast* with Brian McDonald

About the Author

Jessie Kwak is an author, ghostwriter, and freelance marketing copywriter living in Portland, Oregon. As a writer, she sends readers on their own journeys to immersive worlds filled with fascinating characters, gunfights, and dinner parties. When she's not raving about her latest favorite sci-fi series to her friends, she can be found sewing, mountain biking, or out exploring new worlds both at home and abroad. She is the author of supernatural thriller *From Earth and Bone*, the Bulari Saga series of gangster sci-fi novels, and productivity guide *From Chaos to Creativity*. You can learn more about her at www.jessiekwak.com or follow her on Twitter (@jkwak).

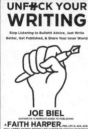